DAD FOOD

ABOUT THE AUTHOR

Dylan McGrath is one of Ireland's best-known chefs and one of the youngest Irish chefs to achieve a Michelin star. He is the proprietor of several well-known Dublin restaurants, a brother and a dad. Dylan was a judge on *MasterChef Ireland* and had his own popular TV show, *Dylan McGrath's Secret Service*, which taught individuals from marginalised backgrounds kitchen skills and was described by the *Irish Times* as 'a show [that comes] from a place of enormous kindness'. His mission to help get Ireland's dads cooking comes from that same place.

DAD FOOD

BIG, BOLD FLAVOURS
FOR EVERYDAY EATING

Dylan McGrath

GILL BOOKS

Gill Books

Hume Avenue
Park West
Dublin 12
www.gillbooks.ie

Gill Books is an imprint of M.H. Gill and Co.

© Dylan McGrath 2024
9781804580851

Designed by www.grahamthew.com
Photography by Leo Byrne
Food styling by Orla Neligan
Edited by Orla Broderick
Printed and bound by Printer Trento, Italy
This book is typeset in Covik Sans.

The paper used in this book comes from the wood pulp of
sustainably managed forests.

A CIP catalogue record for this book is available from the British
Library.

5 4 3 2 1

To my mother, Mary, who didn't live long enough
to see the dads we became.

CONTENTS

INTRODUCTION

WELCOME TO DAD FOOD

This cookery book is not just about recipes – it's a celebration of the special bond between fathers and their children, and it takes place in the heart of the home: the kitchen. I hope to encourage you to take on these achievable recipes, while also creating great cooking memories with your loved ones.

To the fathers who choose to challenge themselves, I hope you will see that cooking for others isn't just about preparing meals but can also be about making memories, fostering creativity or teaching valuable life skills – and these recipes are easy to follow, with plenty of opportunities for little hands to get involved.

Each section provides new flavoursome ideas, depending on the meal time or cooking task you have at hand. Cooking from this book will hopefully set you on a culinary journey that will nourish both body and soul, while also strengthening the bonds of family. So get ready to cook, create and connect with your kids in the most delicious way possible.

THE FOOD

Food is such an important part of our everyday life, and what we put into our bodies can really affect how we feel, how we look and how we operate. To some, food is merely fuel – to others, it's an essential indulgence to take time over and pleasure in. Over the years, my relationship with food has changed. As a chef, it was very much based around my obsession with flavour, constantly considering how something smelt, how it tasted and the harmony of the ingredients in the mouth and on the plate. But as a father, I more often think of how I can get it onto the table quick and hot, mostly because of my busy lifestyle, which I'm sure most of us can relate to. So my choices as a father are simpler in their approach, but I still want things to taste great. Food at home is different from food in a restaurant – the equipment is not the same, the kitchen space is not the same, and time always seems a factor when preparing meals at home. But the effort we put into a dish or a big meal should hopefully translate to the enjoyment felt by our loved ones, and having a bunch of go-to recipes that are achievable in the home kitchen and packed with flavour is what this book is all about. I encourage you to taste as you go and trust your instincts – the difference between good food and great food is being curious and always tasting and adjusting.

COOKING WITH CHILDREN

Far be it from me to be teaching anyone about parenting – I can only share my experiences, my optimism and my hope for the future. So much data is available to us today on parenting and how best to approach it, but one thing is clear: we know more about the importance of a dad's role in a child's life, and numerous studies show that it's a central part of building self-esteem in children. Modern parenting can prove challenging for many reasons, with people finding themselves in all sorts of situations. I believe that food is a great way to connect with your children and family members, regardless of the circumstances. Taking the time to prepare a meal that far exceeds everyone's expectations, or better still, involving the children in the preparation, is a great way to connect.

Cooking together provides an opportunity for you as a dad or male role model to spend quality time with your little ones. It encourages communication by creating a relaxed environment where you can talk about everyday stuff while working together towards a common goal. Cooking is also a necessary life skill, and by involving your children you can help them develop their skills in following instructions, measuring ingredients and doing things the right way, while also, hopefully, having fun. It can be a creative outlet for you and your kids, encouraging you both to try new recipes, experiment with new flavours and fire your imaginations.

Not everyone has a biological father in their life, and children often have other male role models. If you have children in your life, and you are in this position, this book is for you as well. Cooking with kids can be a meaningful way to connect with them and create lasting memories that will strengthen your relationship with them for years to come.

DADS WHO COOK

Some dads cook, but not all do, and I hope that this book can inspire more to try. There is something so rewarding about taking the time to cook food that can be enjoyed by the people we love – doing something thoughtful that brings pleasure to those we care about. For me, pleasing people close to me through food is so enriching. Fathers come from all kinds of backgrounds and different circumstances, but the fundamentals remain the same: good men care about their loved ones, the people who rely on them, and want the best for them. One sure way to communicate this can be through the unselfish act of cooking, hustling up something delicious – it's great way of showing affection and bonding with your children and loved ones that will be appreciated and remembered. Sharing the experience of preparing a meal and then sitting down and enjoying the fruits of your labour can strengthen your relationships and create a great sense of closeness through the harmony of food.

PREPARATION IS KEY

Cooking can be a therapeutic way of unwinding and should not stress you out. But it will take a little time, effort and patience to build your skills and learn the steps to take to ensure success. Get a decent chopping knife, a good board and a sturdy apron that you can use again and again. Try to work clean, keeping a spray disinfectant on hand to help you clean as you go. The more organised you are, the more you'll enjoy the work. Take the time to buy ingredients that you're happy with, read the recipe at least twice, and then follow the instructions. Putting something hot and full of flavour on the table is easier said than done, but like most things in life, making the effort is half the battle! So whether you're an avid cook or just trying some recipes out for the first time, enjoy the process and the rest will fall into place.

HOW TO USE THIS BOOK

There are a few core recipes in this book – building blocks that allow you to make different dishes – in the jars section. Making these means you'll be able to make several dishes, depending on the time of day or the mood you're in – for example, the pear and shallot chutney is in a number of recipes, as is the granola, and the honey roast garlic raises its head a few times too. These are good staples that you can add in regularly when you choose to cook.

I have included an equipment section to indicate the types of gadgets you can collect on your culinary journey – perfect also for requesting for birthdays and Christmas! They will make your cooking easier and more enjoyable – better equipment will have better results.

The recipes also have symbols indicating their difficulty, from easy to more of a challenge (one chef's hat to three), so you can track your progress through the book. I believe that, with a little focus, everything in this book is achievable but some skills take a little time. Hopefully you will use these recipes again and again as you develop those skills – there's plenty here to take your cooking in different directions and something for everyone. And finally, remember that the beauty of doing the cooking and taking on the role of chef is that it's always helpful when negotiating about who's doing the washing-up!

THE KITCHEN KIT

AIR FRYER

A number of these are on the market at different strengths. I like the double-compartment ones, and Ninja is the brand I am most comfortable with.

BAKING TINS

Get a few different sizes of tins – good non-stick ones are easily available these days.

BENCH SCALE

I like to use something electronic, as it's more precise and can do small measures. Get one that converts into grams, fluid ounces and ounces.

BLENDER

It's a really good idea to invest in a solid blender. I recommend Hamilton Beach for a domestic kitchen.

CHARGRILL PAN

There are a few varieties of these on the market. The trick is to get them really hot so they're smoking before you char any of your meat or vegetables.

CHOPPING BOARD

A good chopping board is important. I like to use a thick wooden one. Keep it clean with a sanitiser and oil it once in a while.

CHOPPING KNIFE

Get yourself a good chopping knife with a handle that's comfortable to hold. Japanese knives are great, but I recommend you start with the German Wüsthof – it's a great beginner's knife.

COFFEE GRINDER

These are great for doing small amounts of blending, normally for spices or dried herbs. They have good motors and are very fast.

FOOD PROCESSOR

I recommend a processor with a 1 litre capacity. These are great for making butters or blitzing half portions of the soup recipes or the smoothies.

FRYING PAN

I like to use an old-school thick black cast-iron pan or skillet. The thicker the pan the better the chance of crisping because of the retention of heat. Frying pans like this can be thrown into the oven as well without melting.

HAND BLENDER

Modern hand blenders are very easy, accessible and quick. We use them in the restaurant kitchens a lot, perfect for cream. Not as strong as a stand-up blender but they definitely have their uses.

JAPANESE MANDOLIN

These are an excellent piece of kit. You can get them online or in an Asian supermarket. Use the guard and watch your fingers. These slice so fine – they're perfection.

KAMADO EGG BARBECUE

These are an advanced piece of kit, but the smaller one will fit out the back of most houses. They're good because you can really control the heat, as well as achieve that excellent char and smoky flavour by pulling down the lid. They are very powerful when held at the right temperature.

KITCHEN BLOWTORCH

Essential for giving that crisp caramel top on your brûlée or simply adding a charred flavour to your vegetables.

KITCHEN SCISSORS

I find these very helpful for prepping fish or chicken.

KITCHEN THERMOMETER

This is brilliant for sugar work or checking if meat is cooked – they'll do most jobs. You'll get them online, and do invest in a good one.

MASHER

An old-school potato masher with a solid handle, made of metal and with small grooves to get into the corners of the pot is essential in every kitchen.

MICROPLANE

These are essential in most kitchens – us chefs love them. They're a kind of fine grater that releases the oils in a fine way, rather than in big chunks, releasing better flavour. Use them for zesting fruit and grating nuts or cheese.

MEASURING JUG

I'd go metal here, though you could use Pyrex. An essential for measuring fluids.

MOULI AND DRUM SIEVE

If you want to go the extra mile with your mash to ensure absolutely no lumps, buy a potato Mouli. Once the mash has passed through that, get a scraper and pass it through a drum sieve.

NINJA BLENDER

These normally come with a few different attachments, allowing you to make purées, smoothies and grind spices. These are very good, powerful, reliable and safe with supervised little ones.

NINJA WOODFIRE ELECTRIC OUTDOOR OVEN

I've made good pizzas in this compact oven. It gets really hot and is a very practical piece of kit for the home, with lots of exciting recipes to try.

NON-STICK PAN

Something between 20 and 30cm is ideal. These are great for eggs, fish, omelettes and crêpes – they're so versatile. Just wipe the pan out with a cloth when you're finished – don't put them in the dishwasher. They'll last longer.

NUTRIBULLET

Great for making smoothies, curries or soups – so fast and strong, they're one of my favourite appliances.

OONI PIZZA OVEN

These are great for the back garden and reach a fantastic heat. They produce really nice pizzas, but they cook quickly so you need to keep an eye on them, and it's better to keep the dough thin.

PASTRY BRUSH

Keep a separate brush in the kitchen for brushing on oil, melted butter or egg wash – one that's just for this job and you don't use for anything else.

PERFORATED SERVING SPOON

This is an ideal kitchen utensil – great for poached eggs and getting blanched vegetables out of hot water.

RUBBER SPATULA

These are perfect for scraping any bowl or pan with no waste. They're easy to hold and get into all those corners. An excellent present.

SILICON BAKING MATS

Us chefs love these. No mess, very effective and non-stick – all you need from a baking mat.

STAINLESS-STEEL MIXING BOWL

I like to have a few of these of different sizes.

STAND MIXER

For a domestic kitchen, I recommend a KitchenAid – they're neat, compact, have a good engine and have enough attachments for the different jobs needed.

WIRE RACKS

These are very important when cooling down breads or meats. Getting your product up off the hot tray and on to the rack allows it to cool that bit quicker so the bottom doesn't

WOODEN SPOONS

There are plenty of these in most kitchens, but they're still the best for stirring pots because they don't conduct heat. In my day, mums would use these as a weapon!

BREAKFAST

AND

BRUNCH

Many of us want to indulge at the weekend –
maybe not watch the calories so much – and
we might have a bit more time to spend cooking.
I would encourage you to purchase your
ingredients midweek and then allocate an hour
on Saturday or Sunday morning to do a decent
breakfast or brunch. These recipes could be as
big a hit in your house as they are in mine.
I've tried to keep them simple enough in terms
of technique but still packing in as much
flavour as possible.

SPICY RÖSTI

2 large Rooster potatoes
  (about 500g)
1 tsp Chinese five-spice
  powder
1 tsp smoked paprika
1 tsp ras el hanout
1 tsp onion powder
60g duck fat
60g butter
20g potato flour
vegetable oil, for deep-frying
salt and freshly ground white
  pepper

SERVES 2–4

This is really just a spicy hash brown, fried in a couple of spoonfuls of duck fat along with some butter. The key is to squeeze the starch from the potatoes, so you end up with a super-crispy result, and to make sure the oil is hot enough, so it isn't absorbed. Perfect with pear and shallot chutney (page 240) and some fried eggs.

Prepare the potatoes · Preheat the oven to 220°C (425°F/Gas Mark 7). Peel the potatoes, then coarsely grate using the largest side of a box grater. Do not store the grated potato in water or wash it – the sticky starch is vital to this recipe. Instead, put the potato into a clean tea towel, fold the towel around it to form a ball, and squeeze as hard as you can to remove as much moisture as possible. Put the potato into a bowl and mix in the spices. Melt the duck fat and butter in a small pan, then fold into the spicy potato mixture. Spread into a 30cm × 25cm shallow baking tin in an even layer.

Cook the potatoes · Roast the rösti for 12–14 minutes, until the potato is just cooked but still firm. Remove from the oven and very gently mix through the potato flour and season with salt and pepper. Be gentle with the mixture – try not to break up the strands of potatoes.

Shape the rösti · Line a 20cm × 15cm baking tin that is at least 5cm deep with parchment paper and add the potato mixture in an even layer, making sure the corners are just as deep and pressing it down firmly with the back of a spoon. The depth of the rösti must be an even 5cm all over. Cover with another sheet of parchment paper and put another tray on top, then press with a weight (a few tin cans will do the trick) and chill overnight.

Deep-fry the rösti · Heat a deep-fat fryer with oil to 180°C (350°F). Remove the rösti mixture from the fridge and take off the weights, extra tray and layer of parchment, then cut into 6–8 roughly 100g portions. Fry the rösti in a couple of batches until they are crisp and golden brown – this will take about 3–4 minutes. Remove each batch and drain on kitchen paper. Season with a little extra salt, if liked, and serve immediately.

THE GREAT SAUSAGE SANDWICH

2 tbsp olive oil

2 pork and leek sausages

4 tbsp caramelised onion
marmalade (page 234)

4 tsp softened butter

2 thick slices white sourdough
bread (cut from a large loaf)

50g freshly grated Parmesan

2 eggs

2 slices red Cheddar cheese
(from a packet)

3 tbsp pear and shallot
chutney (page 240)

salt and freshly ground black
pepper

homemade brown sauce (page
229) and triple-cooked chips
(page 174), to serve

SERVES 1

This is perfect for a Saturday morning. Just get some old-fashioned pork sausages, the type that you like, and keep it simple: roast them, then stick them between slices of thick-cut bread, ideally sourdough. The Parmesan gives a nice crust. Make the chutney up in advance – it'll keep for months, and the flavour gets better over time.

Cook the sausages · Preheat the oven to 170°C (325°F/Gas Mark 3). Heat 1 teaspoon of the oil in a small ovenproof frying pan over a high heat and sauté the sausages for a minute or two until golden brown. Transfer to the oven for 6 minutes to finish cooking.

Heat the marmalade · In a separate pan, heat the caramelised onion marmalade over a low heat to warm through, stirring occasionally.

Prepare the bread · Heat a large non-stick frying pan over a medium heat. Spread the butter on both sides of each slice of bread. Sprinkle half of the Parmesan on to the pan, in two circles (one for each slice of bread). Then add the slices on top of the Parmesan circles. Cook until the slices start to colour – a minute is about right. Sprinkle the remaining Parmesan over the uncooked side of each slice, and then flip over. Continue to cook for another minute, until the Parmesan melts and gives a nice golden crust. Transfer to a plate.

Cook the eggs · Keep the frying pan on the heat and give it a quick wipe, then add the rest of the oil and break in the eggs. Season with salt and pepper and cook to your liking, basting the yolks with the oil.

Build the sandwich · Preheat the grill to high. Remove the sausages from the oven and, using a fork to hold them steady, quickly cut into 2cm slices on the diagonal. Spread one slice of bread with the caramelised onion marmalade and add a layer of sausages, then cover with the Cheddar, cutting the slices to fit. Flash under the grill until melted. Meanwhile, spread the other slice of bread with the chutney and, once the cheese has melted, sandwich them both together.

Time to serve · Put the sausage sandwich on a warm serving plate and top with the two fried eggs. Serve with a small dish of homemade brown sauce and some triple-cooked chips.

POACHED EGGS AND SMOKED SALMON WITH MUSTARD BUTTER SAUCE

8 eggs (very fresh)
70g cream
4 tbsp shallot reduction (page 214)
170g unsalted butter, chilled and diced
1 tsp wholegrain mustard
pinch of sugar
4 thick slices sourdough bread
12 slices smoked salmon
salt and freshly ground white pepper
watercress sprigs, to garnish

SERVES 4

The shallot reduction in the butter sauce, finished with a spoonful of wholegrain mustard, is a lovely harmony with the simple smoked salmon and runny poached eggs. The sauce should be used straight away, and you could add some chopped dill or tarragon for a more herby finish.

Poach the eggs · Crack one egg into a small bowl. Bring a large pan of water to the boil, then reduce to a gentle simmer on a low heat. Stir the water to create a gentle whirlpool, which will help the egg white wrap around the yolk, then carefully slide the egg into the water. Quickly repeat with the other eggs. Poach for 3–4 minutes for soft-poached eggs.

Make the mustard butter sauce · Meanwhile, measure the cream and shallot reduction into a small pan, place over a high heat and boil until the liquid has reduced by half, then remove from the heat and whisk in the butter, a little at a time, until the sauce has come together and emulsified. Pass through a fine sieve, then stir in the mustard and add a pinch of sugar. Season to taste.

Time to serve · Gently remove the poached eggs from the water using a slotted spoon and blot any water from the bottom with kitchen paper. Toast the sourdough and put on plates. Arrange the smoked salmon on top of each piece of toast and add the poached eggs. Cover with the sauce and garnish with the watercress to serve.

CRÊPES MANDARIN WITH MASCARPONE AND MARMALADE

FOR THE BATTER

250g plain flour
30g caster sugar, plus extra for dusting
pinch of salt
4 eggs
600ml milk
finely grated zest and juice of 2 mandarins
1 tbsp butter

FOR THE ORANGE MASCARPONE

250g mascarpone cream
50g Seville orange marmalade
finely grated zest of 1 orange

FOR THE SAUCE

30g light brown sugar
40g chilled butter, diced
50g Seville orange marmalade, plus a little extra (optional)
juice of 1 orange
1 tsp vanilla extract
juice of ½ lemon
5 fresh mint leaves, chopped, plus extra sprigs to garnish

1 mandarin, thickly sliced horizontally, to garnish
100g butter (for cooking)

SERVES 4–6

Not as posh as the French Suzette – I've removed the alcohol for kids, but with good marmalade and fresh mandarins it tastes just as good, perfect for an afternoon treat or on Pancake Tuesday. The mascarpone softens the sharpness of the marmalade, and the mint keeps it fresh.

Make the batter · Sift the flour, sugar and salt into a large bowl. Make a well in the centre and break the eggs into it. In a separate bowl, add the milk, mandarin juice and zest and mix. Start whisking the eggs, and then add the milk, mandarin juice and zest mixture. Continue whisking until you have the consistency of single cream. Leave to rest for 30 minutes. Melt 1 tablespoon of butter in a small pan or in the microwave and whisk into the batter.

Make the orange mascarpone · Put the mascarpone in a bowl with the orange marmalade and orange zest. Beat until evenly combined, then cover with cling film and chill until needed.

Make the sauce · Heat a heavy-based pan over a medium heat. Add the brown sugar and heat until the sugar has dissolved. Increase the heat and continue to cook, without stirring, until the mixture has turned to a caramel – swirl the pan occasionally to ensure the mixture caramelises evenly. Reduce the heat, then add the chilled butter and orange marmalade and allow to melt, stirring occasionally. Add the orange juice and vanilla and continue to reduce until syrup-like in texture. Remove from the heat and add the lemon juice and mint. Set aside until needed.

Make the crêpes · Heat a large non-stick frying pan over a medium heat and add a teaspooon of butter to grease the pan. Take a ladleful of the crêpe batter and pour around the bottom of the pan until evenly coated, tipping it around from side to side and pouring off any excess. It should take about 45 seconds to cook on the first side, then flip it over and cook for 30 seconds on the other side. Slide on to a warm plate and dust lightly with sugar, then cook the remainder, adding a little butter for each crêpe. This amount will make 12–14 crêpes in total.

Finish the crêpes · Fold each crêpe in half, adding a little more of the marmalade if you wish, then in half again to form triangles. Warm the sauce in the frying pan, add the folded crêpes and allow to warm through, basting to coat them evenly in the sauce – you may need to do this in batches depending on how many you are serving.

Time to serve · Arrange the crêpes on plates, spooning around the warm sauce. Garnish with the slices of mandarin and add a scoop or quenelle of orange mascarpone to each one. Garnish with mint sprigs.

STRIPLOIN STEAK WITH OVEN-DRIED TOMATOES AND CARAMELISED ONION BUTTER

FOR THE OVEN-DRIED TOMATOES
4 plum tomatoes
pinch of sugar
2 garlic cloves, thinly sliced (on a mandolin)
2 fresh thyme sprigs, leaves stripped
olive oil, for preserving

FOR THE BUTTER
250g butter, at room temperature
150g caramelised onion marmalade (page 234)
120g confit garlic (page 237)
35g white miso
15g fresh tarragon, leaves stripped
30g fresh flat-leaf parsley, leaves stripped

2 × 225–275g striploin steaks
1 tbsp olive oil
150g caramelised onion marmalade (page 234)
salt and freshly ground black pepper
fresh watercress tossed in extra virgin olive oil and lemon, to garnish

SERVES 2

Give yourself a bit more time here for the tomatoes because they're cooked low and slow. But once they're done, they'll keep for weeks. The key to this dish is picking a good steak, and the miso in the butter adds an umami note as it melts onto the meat for an extra layer of deliciousness. This is a very substantial weekend breakfast, but it would also make a fantastic main for lunch or dinner.

Cook the tomatoes · Preheat the oven to 110°C (220°F/Gas Mark ¼). Cut the tomatoes into quarters and remove the seeds with your fingers, keeping the membrane. Put in a bowl, then add a pinch of salt with the sugar, garlic and thyme, tossing well to coat. Arrange the tomato quarters on a grill rack set into a baking tin and dry out in the oven for 1½–2 hours, until they have shrunk by a third. Leave to cool, then transfer to a jar and pour over enough olive oil to cover. Set aside until needed.

Make the butter · Put the butter in a food processor and add the caramelised onions, confit garlic, miso and herbs with 2 teaspoons of salt and ½ teaspoon of pepper. Blend to combine, then put in a bowl and set aside at room temperature until needed.

Cook the steaks · When you're ready to eat, put a large heavy-based frying pan over a high heat. Rub the steaks with oil and then season with salt and pepper. Add to the pan and cook for 2–3 minutes on each side for medium rare (55°C) – 60°C for medium, 65°C for medium well and 70°C for well done if you have a thermometer to check.

Time to serve · Warm the caramelised onion marmalade in a pan and then divide between warm serving plates. Top each one with a cooked steak, then add two pieces of the oven-dried tomatoes and cover them with a big spoonful of the flavoured butter (the remainder can be used another time and can be frozen). Garnish with the dressed watercress to serve.

HEALTHY

CHOICES

We are all concerned about our children's health and well-being, and the food we give them is a great way of ensuring that they're getting what they need as well as introducing them to new experiences. The recipes in this section are ones you can depend on to get some nutrients and goodness into your little ones. While healthy choices are often associated with unappealing flavours, I believe it doesn't have to be that way. Even healthy choices should taste great, and making them together, fresh, is a great opportunity to introduce your kids to things they wouldn't normally try. So here, with very little cooking, are some simple, nutritious options that taste good – and they're not just for the kids, but also for the dads, who need high energy to do an effective job. I have also included the calorie counts for the recipes in this section for those who want to use them.

SMOOTHIES

A quick and simple smoothie is perfect in the morning or afternoon. And, made with fresh fruit, it's a great way to get some good nutrients into your loved ones.

STRAWBERRY, BANANA AND RASPBERRY SMOOTHIE

100g strawberries
1 large banana
120g raspberries
200g plain natural yoghurt
1 tsp honey
100ml oat milk (or use another milk if you prefer)
10 ice cubes

MAKES 2 GLASSES
270KCAL PER GLASS

Make the smoothie · Trim the stalks off the strawberries and place in a blender or NutriBullet. Peel the banana and add to the blender with the raspberries, yoghurt, honey and oat milk. Add the ice cubes and blend until smooth. Serve immediately in tall glasses.

PEANUT BUTTER AND BANANA GRANOLA SMOOTHIE

2 bananas
120ml coconut milk
2 heaped tbsp crunchy peanut butter
1 tsp maple syrup
60g the best granola (see page 27)
10 ice cubes

MAKES 2 GLASSES
381KCAL PER GLASS

Make the smoothie · Peel the bananas and place in a blender or NutriBullet. Add the coconut milk, peanut butter, maple syrup, granola and ice cubes and blend until smooth. Serve immediately in tall glasses.

JUICES

Not everyone has a juicer, although I recommend investing in even a small one. Maybe hint at one for a birthday present or Christmas. It's a great way of getting the goodness we need in the morning. If you're having a more indulgent breakfast, juices can be a clean and fresh way to start the day. I've kept it simple here and relied on flavours that work well together. They are also quick and easy – they take seconds to knock up and then you just pour them over ice.

THE GREEN PUNCH

½ pineapple
2 red apples
1 cucumber
2 kiwi fruit, peeled
50g baby spinach leaves
6 fresh mint sprigs
ice cubes, to serve

MAKES 2 GLASSES
181KCAL PER GLASS

Make the juice · Cut the pineapple half into quarters and then cut off the core and skin. Place in a juicer with the rest of the ingredients and serve immediately in tall glasses over ice.

THE DETOX

20g piece fresh root ginger
500g carrots
2 red apples
4 fresh tarragon sprigs
ice cubes, to serve

MAKES 2 GLASSES
254KCAL PER GLASS

Make the juice · Put all the ingredients, except the ice, into a juicer, then serve immediately in tall glasses over the ice.

FRUITY CLEANSE

4 green apples
20g piece fresh root ginger
3 raw medium beetroot
ice cubes, to serve

MAKES 2 GLASSES
168KCAL PER GLASS

Make the juice · Place all the ingredients, except the ice, into a juicer, then serve immediately in tall glasses over the ice.

THE BEST GRANOLA

250g raw mixed nuts, coarsely
  chopped
250g porridge oats
1 tsp ground cinnamon
1 tsp ground allspice
pinch of sea salt
2 tbsp maple syrup
2 tsp olive oil
1 tbsp vanilla extract
125g dried apricots, chopped
125g coconut flakes
2 tbsp cacao nibs

MAKES 800G
386KCAL PER 80G

There are lots of granola recipes out there, but for me it's about flavour as well as goodness, and this recipe has both. It might mean a trip to the health food shop, but you should be able to get most of the ingredients in the supermarket. There's a bit of back and forth in the oven, but once made it'll keep for ages in a dry place. You can put it on so many things – it's well worth the effort.

Mix the granola · Preheat the oven to 120°C (250°F/Gas Mark ½). Combine the nuts, oats, spices and salt in a large bowl. Drizzle over the maple syrup, oil and vanilla and mix well.

Cook the granola · Spread the granola out in a baking tray and bake for 15 minutes. Remove from the oven and give everything a good stir. Rotate the baking tray and bake for another 15 minutes.

Finish the granola · Take the granola out of the oven, stir in the apricots and cook for 5 minutes. Scatter over the coconut flakes and cook for a final 2 minutes. Remove from the oven and stir in the cacao nibs. Leave to cool.

Store the granola · Transfer the granola to an airtight jar. It will keep well for up to 1 month. Use as required.

GRANOLA BARS

60g flaked almonds
100g maple syrup
50g butter
30g xylitol (sugar substitute)
160g dark chocolate chips
250g the best granola (page 27)

MAKES 8-10 BARS
265KCAL PER 100G
🍞 🍞 🍞

Here's a fun way of using up more of the granola by making homemade healthy snacks. These bars should be taken out of the fridge before cutting and served at room temperature so they're chewy but still a little crunchy.

Roast the almonds · Preheat the oven to 180°C (350°F/Gas Mark 4). Place the flaked almonds on a baking tray and roast for 10 minutes. Turn the oven down to 110°C (225°F/Gas Mark ¼).

Make the bars · In a pot, melt the maple syrup with the butter and xylitol. Take off the heat, then add 100g of dark chocolate and mix well. Leave it to cool for five minutes. In a bowl, add 30g of dark chocolate to the granola, then pour in the slightly cooled mixture from the pot and mix well. Line a 35 × 25cm baking tray with parchment paper. Spread the roasted almonds on it, add 30g of dark chocolate and place in the oven for 2 minutes, till the chocolate melts. Then spread the granola mix on top and leave in the fridge to set for 1 hour.

Time to serve · Before serving, remove from the fridge for 30 minutes. Then turn out of the tin, and cut into 8–10 bars and serve at room temperature.

LEMON YOGHURT WITH GRANOLA AND BLUEBERRIES

300g Greek strained yoghurt
    (10% fat)
finely grated zest and juice of
    1 lemon
45–65ml vanilla stock syrup
    (page 254)
2 tsp vanilla extract
200g blueberries
2 fresh mint leaves (optional)
2 spoonfuls of the best
    granola (page 27)

SERVES 2
236KCAL PER SERVING

Kitchen Note: For best results, I recommend using vanilla stock syrup here, but if you don't have it, you could replace it with a spoonful of caster sugar or honey in the yoghurt and 2 tablespoons of honey in the dressed blueberries.

This can be made in advance and served in the morning or after dinner as a treat. The granola adds some crunch and spice to the fruit and yoghurt. Feel free to use other berries or yoghurts with higher fat content or lower sugar, depending on your diet.

Flavour the yoghurt · Put the yoghurt in a bowl and stir in the lemon zest and juice. Add enough of the vanilla stock syrup to taste (25ml for not too sweet and 45ml if you prefer it more sweet) along with the vanilla extract.

Make the dressed blueberries · In a separate bowl, mix the blueberries with 20ml of the vanilla stock syrup. Thinly slice the mint leaves into batons, if using, and fold into the blueberries.

Time to serve · Divide the lemon yoghurt between two glasses. Leave to chill in the fridge for 15 minutes, and then spoon the dressed blueberries on top. Finally, scatter over the granola to serve.

ORANGE, APPLE, FENNEL AND AVOCADO SALAD

2 oranges (I like one to be a
   blood orange)
1 firm, ripe avocado
1 apple
1 fennel bulb
6–8 tbsp orange yoghurt
   dressing (see page 245)
handful rocket and watercress,
   well picked over

SERVES 4
216KCAL PER SERVING

**Introducing your children to vegetables can be tricky – I find it easier
if you pair it with a little fruit. Here I've used two fruits and two raw,
crunchy vegetables, together with a little fresh orange dressing, that I
hope you like as much as we do.**

Prepare the oranges · Using a sharp knife, slice a little off the top and
bottom of the oranges to give a stable cutting surface. Using the front of the
knife, starting at the top, slice downwards, following the curve of the fruit.
Cut away all the skin and pith, ensuring not to remove any flesh, then using a
mandolin or a knife cut into ½cm slices.
Prepare the rest of the fruit · Cut the avocado in half and peel off the skin,
then using a mandolin or knife cut into ½cm slices. Cut the apple into ½cm
slices.
Make the salad · Trim the fennel and, again using the mandolin or sharp
knife, cut into 1mm thin slices. Arrange the orange, avocado and fennel on a
serving plate, and drizzle over enough of the dressing to lightly coat. Scatter
the rocket and watercress on top. Serve immediately.

BONE BROTH

2 beef bones (ask your butcher for two large beef knuckles)
500g pork belly, cut into 4cm squares
500g chicken wings
5 smoked bacon rashers
2 carrots, cut into big chunks
2 leeks, cut into big chunks
1 onion, cut into big chunks
3 celery sticks, cut into big strips
100ml vegetable oil
4 bay leaves
1 tbsp white peppercorns
1 tbsp coriander seeds
5 cardamon pods

MAKES ABOUT 1 LITRE

Some dads I know from the gym tell me they make a batch of this at the weekend and drink it throughout the week. It's packed with goodness and very nourishing, and you can freeze it or keep it fresh. Add some noodles, spring onions, a fried egg and a bit of pork and you have a simple ramen. I've added a few bones here to give it real depth of flavour.

Boil the bones · Preheat the oven to 230°C (450°F/Gas Mark 8). Put the beef bones in a large pan and cover with cold water. Bring to the boil over a high heat and simmer for 10–15 minutes, then remove the bones and keep warm, reserving the liquid.

Make the broth · Put the warm bones in a roasting tin with the pork belly, chicken wings, rashers, vegetables and oil. Give everything a good mix and roast for 30 minutes. Remove from the oven and add the bones, vegetables and meats to the reserved water. Add the herbs and spices and bring to the boil, then simmer for 4–5 hours. Skim and discard the impurities that rise to the top during cooking. Strain, chill and use as required. The broth keeps for 3 months in the freezer and 4–5 days in the fridge.

SNACKS

Here are a bunch of simple recipes that can be made with kids. Some of them are sweet and some of them are savoury, but they're all fun, approachable and familiar. They're quick enough to put together and the ingredients are easily sourced – just little twists on familiar snacks we all know and love. The kids will certainly enjoy them, and you can create some good memories putting them together.

PEANUT CARAMEL POPCORN

250g caster sugar
150g dry roasted peanuts
2 tbsp sunflower oil
120g freshly made popcorn
   (still warm – made in the
   microwave or a pan)
4 tsp salted caramel butter
   sauce (see page 250)

SERVES 6–8

The saltiness of the peanuts is great with the caramel and popcorn – perfect for a Friday-night treat. Make the caramel on your own and get the kids to help with the rest, after it has cooled down.

Make the caramel · Heat a heavy-based pan over a medium heat. Add the sugar and heat until the sugar has dissolved. Increase the heat and continue to cook, without stirring, until the mixture has turned to a golden-brown caramel – swirl the pan occasionally to ensure the mixture caramelises evenly. Add the peanuts and stir in.

Make the peanut brittle · Grease a silicone baking mat or parchment-lined tray with the sunflower oil and pour the caramel on it. Leave to cool down and harden, then blitz to a powder in a coffee grinder. This amount will make 400g and is enough for about four batches of this recipe. Store the remainder in an airtight jar in a cool place for up to a week.

Time to serve · Tip the warm popcorn into a bowl and add six heaped tablespoons of the peanut brittle powder, along with the salted caramel butter sauce, stirring to coat evenly. Serve immediately.

WHITE CHOCOLATE FUDGE WITH SALTED PEANUTS

265g white chocolate drops
100ml cream
190g smooth peanut butter
100ml warm water
50g salted jumbo peanuts,
   halved

**MAKES 20–30 FUDGE
PIECES**

**This is the easiest fudge, with just a few ingredients, and it has a
lovely texture.**

Melt the chocolate · Put the chocolate drops in a large bowl over a pan of
simmering water to melt. Remove the bowl from the heat and, using a spatula,
stir until smooth.

Make the fudge · Put the cream into a small heavy-based pan over a medium
heat and bring to the boil. Add the cream and the peanut butter to the melted
chocolate and whisk until smooth. Add the water and whisk.

Set the fudge · Line a 500g loaf tin with parchment paper and pour in the
fudge, smoothing down the surface with a spatula. Leave to cool and then
place in the fridge for 1 hour to set.

Time to serve · When the fudge is set, lift it out of the tin and peel off the
parchment paper. Cut into rectangles and press a peanut half into each
one. These will keep in an airtight container in a cool place for 2–3 weeks,
separated with layers of parchment paper, or can be used straight away.

LIME MARSHMALLOWS WITH CHOCOLATE, COCONUT AND LIME DIPPING SAUCE

FOR THE MARSHMALLOWS

14 gelatine leaves
500ml water
700g caster sugar
2 tbsp liquid glucose
3 egg whites
finely grated zest of 1 lime
vegetable oil, for greasing
100g icing sugar
4 tbsp cornflour

FOR THE SAUCE

60g coconut flakes
280ml coconut milk
60ml cream
150g dark chocolate drops
40ml lime juice and zest of 1 lime

MAKES ABOUT 25 LARGE MARSHMALLOWS

♟ ♟ ♟

Cut these as big as you want! They can also be toasted on summer evenings on the barbecue – and with the hot chocolate, coconut and lime sauce, they're very moreish.

Soften the gelatine · Put the gelatine into a deep bowl and cover with 200ml of the water to soften.

Make the syrup · Put the caster sugar, liquid glucose and the remaining 300ml of water in a large heavy-based pan. Cook over a medium to high heat until the mixture reaches 130°C on a sugar thermometer. Take the pan off the heat, then add the gelatine mixture and carefully stir until dissolved. Be careful, as this mixture can bubble up and spit. Carefully pour into a heatproof jug.

Make the marshmallows · Using a stand mixer, whisk the egg whites in a large heatproof bowl until soft peaks form. Keep whisking while you slowly pour in the warm syrup in a thin, steady stream. Keep beating for 20 minutes until the mixture is smooth, noticeably thicker and cool. Fold in the lime zest.

Set the marshmallow · Line a 25cm × 35cm roasting tin or dish with parchment and brush with oil. Mix together the icing sugar and cornflour, then sieve a third of it into the tin or dish to coat the inside. Pour in the marshmallow mixture, level with a spatula, then leave to set for 3 hours.

Cut the marshmallow · Spread a large piece of parchment paper on your counter and sieve over another third of the cornflour and sugar mixture. Turn the set marshmallow out onto the large piece of parchment and peel off the parchment that had lined the tin. Dust the marshmallow and a large, sharp knife with some more of the cornflour sugar mixture. Cut the marshmallows into 5cm × 7cm rectangles, sieving a little cornflour and sugar mixture over each cut side and the knife as you go to prevent them from sticking.

Make the dipping sauce · Preheat your oven to 160°C (325°F/Gas Mark 3). Spread the coconut flakes in an even layer on a baking tray and cook for 8–12 minutes until they're golden-brown. Meanwhile, bring the coconut milk and cream to a simmer in a pan over a medium heat, but do not allow it to boil. Remove from the heat, and stir in the toasted coconut flakes, chocolate drops and lime juice and zest.

Time to serve · Pour the sauce into serving bowls and serve alongside the marshmallows, ready for dipping. You can blowtorch the marshmallows or toast them over a barbecue or a campfire. The marshmallows will keep in an airtight container for up to 2 weeks in a cool place, separated with layers of parchment paper.

HOMEMADE HONEYCOMB

vegetable oil, for greasing
200g caster sugar
100g golden syrup
2 tsp bicarbonate of soda

MAKES A 1 LITRE JAR

I think it's best to make this on your own because it gets very hot, but it's definitely worth it. Break it into large pieces and store it in a jar, then break it into smaller chunks and put it in ice cream or just eat it on its own. It reminds me of my childhood in Belfast.

Prepare the tin · Line a 20cm square tin with parchment paper and brush with oil.

Make the caramel · Place the sugar and golden syrup into a large heavy-based pan over a low heat and cook gently until melted. Try not to let the mixture bubble until the sugar grains have disappeared. Once completely melted, turn up the heat a little and simmer until you have an amber-coloured caramel, which will not take very long. Ideally, check the temperature with a sugar thermometer – it needs to be 136°C (277°F).

Make the honeycomb · Switch off the heat, sprinkle over the bicarbonate of soda and beat with a wooden spoon until it has all disappeared and the mixture is foaming. Take care, as the caramel will react to the bicarbonate of soda and froth up a lot. Scrape into the tin immediately – again, be careful, as the mixture will still be very hot.

Set the honeycomb · The mixture will continue bubbling in the tin, so leave it for at least an hour, until it has become firm and is ready to snap into chunks. Trim it down and cut into long chunks and store both the chunks and trimmings stacked up in a 1 litre jar at room temperature for up to 1 week.

HOMEMADE LEMONADE

1 litre vanilla stock syrup
   (page 254)
6–8 lemons (you need 200ml
   lemon juice)
400ml sparkling water
20-30 ice cubes
handful of fresh mint leaves

MAKES 1.6 LITRES

Homemade lemonade is simple but quite different from what you'll get in the shop. The infusion with lemon zest will keep it tasting super fresh – everybody will appreciate this on a hot summer's day.

Make the lemonade · Put the stock syrup into a large jug. Finely grate the zest from three of the lemons. Peel some long strips of rind from three lemons with a speed peeler and add to the jug. Then squeeze out the juice of all lemons and add to the jug. Stir to combine, cover with cling film and leave in the fridge for 1 hour to infuse.

Time to serve · Add the the sparkling water, ice cubes and mint to the jug, and then pour into glasses. Give each glass a stir with a straw before handing out.

GOOD HOT CHOCOLATE

80ml cream
500ml milk
1 cinnamon stick
½ vanilla pod, split in half and
   seeds scraped out
2 tsp cornflour
50ml water
2 tsp cocoa powder
50g milk or dark chocolate
   drops
lime marshmallows (page 42),
   to decorate

SERVES 2-4

**Good hot chocolate, for me, has decent body and a little spice. This
has both and a generous helping of real chocolate.**

Make the hot chocolate · Put the cream, milk, cinnamon and vanilla pod
and seeds into a heavy-based pan. Bring to the boil, then remove from the
heat and leave to infuse for 10 minutes.

Time to serve · Mix the cornflour in a small dish with the water until
smooth. Whisk the cocoa powder and chocolate dops into the infused liquid,
then whisk in the cornflour mixture. Bring back to the boil, whisking until the
chocolate has melted. Then take out the cinnamon stick and vanilla pod. Blitz
with a hand blender to create a froth. Pour into mugs and top each one with a
lime marshmallow. Caramelise with a blow torch to finish, if you have one, for
an extra flourish.

RASPBERRY, LEMON AND WHITE CHOCOLATE COOKIES

115g butter, at room
  temperature
200g caster sugar
1 egg
1 tsp vanilla extract
zest of 2 lemons
1 tbsp lemon juice
205g plain flour
1 tsp baking powder
1 tsp bicarbonate of soda
150g white chocolate buttons
150g frozen raspberries
vanilla ice cream, to serve

MAKES 8-10

These flavours go really well together. You can make these cookies thick and serve them warm with ice cream, as shown here, or at room temperature with some of our homemade lemonade (page 46).

Make the cookie dough · Put the butter and sugar in a stand mixer with a whisk attachment and beat for 5 minutes until light and fluffy. Add the egg, vanilla, lemon zest and juice and whisk again until combined. Sieve in the flour, baking powder and bicarbonate of soda, then fold in until well combined.

Flavour the cookie dough · Roughly chop 50g of the white chocolate buttons and fold into the cookie dough. Break up 90g of the frozen raspberries gently with a sharp knife and carefully fold into the dough, using a spatula, with just a couple of folds. Cover with cling film and chill for 10 minutes.

Bake the cookies · Preheat the oven to 175°C (345°F/Gas Mark 3½). Scoop 120g pieces of the cookie dough out on to parchment-lined baking trays, keeping them spaced well apart to allow them to expand. (You could also cook them in a skillet, where they'll join together while baking and can be scooped out to serve.) Press a few of the reserved white chocolate buttons and frozen raspberries into each cookie. Bake for 15 minutes, until the edges are golden brown. Leave on the trays or skillet for at least 5 minutes to cool down.

Time to serve · Eat immediately with vanilla ice cream.

PIGS IN BLANKETS WITH PEAR AND SHALLOT CHUTNEY

vegetable oil, for deep-frying

10 cocktail sausages

5 thin rindless smoked streaky bacon rashers, cut in half

375g packet ready-rolled puff pastry (thawed if frozen)

2 egg yolks mixed with 1 tbsp water (egg wash)

½ tsp fennel seeds

1 tsp sesame seeds

½ tsp black mustard seeds

200g pear and shallot chutney, to serve (page 240)

MAKES 10

These are perfect to get kids involved. They are fun to roll up with the puff pastry and cook relatively quickly so they're great for parties or finger food. Make the chutney once and you'll have it for months.

Deep-fry the sausages · Heat the oil in a deep-fat fryer to 170°C (340°F). Cook the cocktail sausages for 2 minutes until lightly golden. Drain on kitchen paper and leave to cool, then roll each one in half a rasher.

Cook the pigs in blankets · Preheat the oven to 200°C (400°F/Gas Mark 6). Unroll the puff pastry and cut into 10 triangles with 4cm sides and 10cm bases. Brush with the egg wash and, starting at the base, roll up each rasher-covered sausage into a croissant shape. Brush again with the egg wash and sprinkle with the fennel, sesame and mustard seeds. Arrange on a parchment-lined baking tray and bake for 20 minutes until crisp and golden brown.

Time to serve · Arrange the pigs in blankets on a warm platter with a dish of pear and shallot chutney or homemade brown sauce (page 229).

FAST

AND

SLOW

SOUPS

This selection of soups is all based around flavour and texture, with some soups chunky and some smooth – investing in a good jug blender will be worthwhile here. For some vegetables, slow cooking produces the best flavour, but with others, cooking them quickly extracts even more flavour – it really depends on the vegetable. Homemade soups are a great way of providing the nutrients kids need, and if you follow the guidance in these recipes and season your soups well, both you and your little ones will love eating them too.

ROASTED CAULIFLOWER SOUP WITH CHEDDAR CROUTONS

50ml olive oil
1 cauliflower, cut into quarters
6 garlic cloves, peeled, plus 1
    extra for the croutons
2 fresh thyme sprigs
150g butter
1 large onion, sliced
400ml chicken stock (from a
    stock cube)
350ml milk, plus a little extra
    if necessary
230ml cream
1 tbsp sea salt
1 tbsp sugar
1 small French baguette, sliced
    into 1cm slices
extra virgin olive oil, for
    drizzling and garnish
50g mature Cheddar, finely
    grated
finely chopped fresh chives, to
    garnish

SERVES 4–6

I would not have gone near cauliflower when I was young, but now I know it's the things that we put with it and the way we serve it that makes it appetising, so here I've roasted the cauliflower and served it with cheesy croutons (which just might have changed my mind as a kid)! It's important that you blitz the soup until it's super smooth.

Start the soup base · Preheat the oven to 160°C (325°F/Gas Mark 3). Heat a large ovenproof frying pan over a medium to high heat. Add half the olive oil and sauté the cauliflower with 3 cloves of garlic and 1 sprig of thyme for 8–10 minutes until golden brown on all sides. Add the butter to the pan with the cauliflower and heat until foaming, then baste until evenly coated. Transfer to the oven for 10–12 minutes until completely tender.

Cook the soup · Meanwhile, heat another heavy-based pan over a low heat. Add the rest of the olive oil, 3 cloves of garlic and the remaining thyme sprig with the onion and sauté for 10–15 minutes until softened and transparent. Add the roasted cauliflower to the onion mixture and then pour in the stock, milk and cream. Season with the sea salt and add the sugar. Bring to a simmer and cook gently for 15 minutes, until piping hot and the flavours have had a chance to combine.

Make the croutons · Arrange the baguette slices on a baking tray and drizzle lightly in extra virgin olive oil. Bake for 15 minutes at 150°C (300°F/Gas Mark 2) to lightly colour. Remove from the oven and rub with a raw garlic clove, then scatter the Cheddar on top and return to the oven for 2 minutes, until the cheese has melted.

Purée the soup · Using a spoon, remove the thyme sprigs from the soup mixture and discard. Transfer the soup to a jug blender and blend until velvety smooth, adding a little more milk if the soup is too thick. Pour back into the pan and gently warm through. Add more milk if you need it.

Time to serve · Ladle the roasted cauliflower soup into bowls, top with a couple of Cheddar croutons, add a sprinkling of chives, then finish with a drizzle of extra virgin olive oil.

ROASTED RED PEPPER AND TOMATO SOUP

2 large red peppers, halved and
  seeds removed
2 ripe tomatoes, quartered
  (skin on)
12 cherry tomatoes
2 fresh thyme sprigs, leaves
  stripped
2 bay leaves
8 garlic cloves, peeled
250ml olive oil
1 large onion, diced
1 tsp coriander seeds
50g tomato purée
400ml vegetable stock (from a
  stock cube)
2 tbsp sugar
4 tbsp crème fraiche
extra virgin olive oil and finely
  chopped fresh chives, to
  garnish
sea salt and freshly ground
  black pepper

SERVES 4

The flavour here comes from the blistering and charring of the pepper and tomato skins when they're roasted in the oven. Once everything is in the pan, it cooks relatively quickly and then goes into the blender to make it really smooth. It just needs a big dollop of crème fraiche then to finish it, or you can use whipped cream to lighten the intensity of the soup. A few slices of focaccia (page 205) with melted mozzarella and pesto would work a treat on the side.

Roast the soup base · Preheat the oven to 200°C (400°F/Gas Mark 6) with a large baking tray in it for 10–15 minutes. Put the peppers, tomatoes, cherry tomatoes, thyme leaves and bay leaves into a large bowl with five of the garlic cloves. Add 100ml of the olive oil with 1 tablespoon of salt and mix well to combine. Pour onto the hot baking tray and roast for 15–20 minutes, until nicely blistered but not burnt.

Finish the soup · Meanwhile, place a heavy-based pan over a low heat. Slice the remaining three garlic cloves. Add the rest of the olive oil and sauté the onion, coriander seeds and sliced garlic for 10–15 minutes, until softened and transparent. Add the tomato purée to the onion mixture and cook for 1 minute. Tip in the roasted vegetables, scraping off all the gooey bits from the bottom of the tray. Cover with the stock and add the sugar and 2 teaspoons of salt and some pepper. Increase the heat and bring to the boil, stirring to combine. Simmer for a few minutes, then remove from the heat and use a blender to blend to a purée. Chill until needed.

Time to serve · Reheat the soup in a pan until warmed through, then check the seasoning. Ladle into bowls and add a tablespoon of crème fraiche to each one. Garnish with a drizzle of extra virgin olive oil and a sprinkling of chives. Add some focaccia toasties alongside, if liked.

MINESTRONE AND BORLOTTI SOUP WITH CHORIZO

300g raw chorizo, skinned and
    diced
3 carrots, diced
3 garlic cloves, finely chopped
2 fresh thyme sprigs, leaves
    removed
1 bay leaf
2 banana shallots, diced
1 red pepper, cored and diced
    roughly
1 yellow pepper, cored and
    diced roughly
4 tbsp tomato purée
4 tsp ras el hanout
200g linguine
4 tbsp extra virgin olive oil,
    plus extra for drizzling
400g tin chopped tomatoes
400ml vegetable stock (from a
    stock cube)
2 × 400g tins borlotti beans,
    drained
3 tbsp sugar
2–3 tbsp basil pesto (see page
    218)
6 cherry tomatoes, halved
4 tbsp freshly grated
    Parmesan
sea salt and freshly ground
    black pepper

SERVES 4

This soup, with all that fried chorizo and cheese, was hugely popular in Rustic Stone when it first opened. There's a good bit of prep for this one, but once you get the ingredients together and cook out the base, the rest is easy. Serve with a big dollop of pesto and you can't go wrong.

Make the soup base · Heat a large heavy-based pan over a medium heat. Add the chorizo and sauté for about 5 minutes until the fat renders out and the chorizo starts to crisp up. Add the carrots, garlic, thyme and bay leaf and sauté for another 3–4 minutes until the carrots have begun to soften. Add the shallots, red and yellow peppers and then stir in the tomato purée and ras el hanout. Cook for 5 minutes, stirring occasionally so that the mixture doesn't catch on the bottom of the pan.

Prepare the pasta · Cook the linguine in a separate pan of boiling salted water for 8 minutes or according to packet instructions. Drain into a colander in the sink, and refresh under cold running water, then dress in 4 tablespoons of oil so it doesn't stick together. Then line the linguine up and cut into 2cm pieces.

Assemble the soup · Add the chopped tomatoes and vegetable stock to the soup base and bring to a simmer, then reduce the heat and cook gently for 20 minutes until slightly reduced. Add the pasta and borlotti beans and sugar and simmer for another 5 minutes to allow the flavours to combine. Season to taste.

Time to serve · Ladle the soup into bowls and spoon on the pesto, then scatter the cherry tomatoes on top. Finish each serving with a generous sprinkling of Parmesan and a good drizzle of olive oil.

WHITE BEAN AND SMOKED BACON SOUP

3 tbsp olive oil
300g streaky bacon lardons
80g butter
1 large onion, thinly sliced
3 garlic cloves, finely chopped
2 fresh thyme sprigs
400g tin cannellini beans (not drained)
400ml chicken stock (from a stock cube)
150ml cream
100ml milk (optional)
80ml extra virgin olive oil, for drizzling
2 tsp finely chopped fresh chives
sea salt and freshly ground white pepper

SERVES 4-6

Because of the smoky bacon flavour, most kids will eat this. Use tinned beans, build the soup and then blitz. And don't forget to keep the crunchy bacon bits for the top.

Cook the bacon · Heat the olive oil in a frying pan over a medium heat. Add the bacon and sauté for about 5 minutes until crispy. Drain on kitchen paper and set 3–4 tablespoons aside to use as a garnish.

Make the soup · Melt the butter in a heavy-based pan over a low heat. Add the onion, garlic and thyme and sauté for 8–10 minutes, until the onion is soft and transparent. Return the crispy bacon to the pan with the cannellini beans, stock and cream. Increase the heat to medium and simmer for 5 minutes. Season to taste. Remove from the heat, take out the thyme and use a jug blender to blend to a smooth purée, adding the milk if you think it's too thick. Chill until needed.

Time to serve · Reheat the soup in a pan over a low heat until warmed through. Be careful that it doesn't stick to bottom of the pan, and then check the seasoning. Ladle into bowls and scatter over the reserved bacon lardons. Drizzle with the extra virgin olive oil and scatter the chives on top.

PISTOU SOUP WITH PINE NUTS AND PARMESAN

100ml extra virgin olive oil

1 onion, grated

2 garlic cloves, grated

2 carrots, grated

1 celery stick, trimmed and grated

1 small fennel bulb, trimmed and grated

1 bay leaf

4 fresh thyme sprigs

150g ditalini (short macaroni) or rigatoni

700ml vegetable stock (from a stock cube)

1 small courgette, trimmed and grated

100g baby broad beans, or fine French green beans cut into small pieces

150g basil pesto, plus extra to garnish (from a jar or use from page 218)

4 tsp roasted pine nuts

50g small cherry tomatoes, halved

4 tsp freshly grated Parmesan

2 tsp chopped fresh flat-leaf parsley

sea salt and freshly ground black pepper

This is a classic, traditional soup. Rather than lots of chopping and dicing, the veg is grated here, just to make it more simple. Serve it with some good olive oil, a little grated Parmesan and a big slice of crusty bread.

Make the soup base · Heat a large heavy-based pan over a medium heat. Add the olive oil and sauté the onion and garlic for 3–4 minutes to soften and sweeten but not colour. Add the carrots, celery, fennel, bay leaf and thyme and sauté for another 3 minutes, until the carrots are beginning to soften.

Prepare the pasta · Cook the pasta in a separate pan of boiling salted water for 8 minutes or according to the packet instructions. Drain and refresh in cold water.

Finish the soup · Pour the vegetable stock into the soup base and bring to a simmer, then cook for 8 minutes. Add the courgette and broad beans and bring back to a simmer, then cook for another minute.

Assemble the soup · Stir the pasta and pesto into the soup, then season to taste and ladle into bowls. Scatter over the pine nuts, cherry tomatoes and Parmesan, then drizzle over a little extra pesto and sprinkle with the parsley.

SERVES 4–6

AIR

FRYER

I've got to admit, the air fryer was a bit of a challenge for me, but these new pieces of equipment have been embraced by many, and I get it. It's all about time and how valuable it is to all of us. I've kept these recipes simple enough, embracing the speed of the air fryer but using techniques to make sure we don't sacrifice any flavour.

LEMON PEPPER CHICKEN SKEWERS

1 lemon
2 garlic cloves, minced
1 tsp garlic powder
1 tsp smoked paprika
2 tsp mild chilli powder
2 tbsp honey, plus 1 tsp for the
  glaze
1 tbsp white peppercorns
good pinch of sea salt flakes
400g skinless and boneless
  chicken thighs, well-
  trimmed and cut in half
  lengthways

SERVES 2

I like to use chicken thighs here, with the skin off so it chars better. These are a little spicy, and the lemon gives it a citrus kick. Marinate as long as you want, but I think an hour is enough.

Marinate the chicken · Finely grate the zest from the lemon and then squeeze the juice from half of it. Put both in a bowl with the fresh garlic and garlic powder, paprika, chilli powder and honey. Put the peppercorns in a pestle and mortar or coffee grinder and crack them down into small pieces. Stir them into the marinade and season with salt. Fold in the chicken and cover the bowl with cling film. Set aside at room temperature for at least 20 minutes, or up to 24 hours in the fridge, to allow the flavours to develop.

Time to cook · Preheat the air fryer to 200°C (400°F). Thread the chicken tightly on to four 20cm bamboo skewers, reserving any marinade. Arrange in the bottom of the air fryer, lined with parchment paper, and cook for 6 minutes, then, using a tongs, turn them over and cook for another 5 minutes until the chicken is cooked through and tender.

Make the glaze · Meanwhile, put the reserved marinade into a small pan with a teaspoon of honey, and reduce for a few minutes to achieve a thick glaze.

Time to serve · When the skewers are cooked, brush liberally with the glaze and arrange two on each warmed serving plate.

CHAR SIU PORK WITH RICE AND FRAGRANT SPINACH

FOR THE PORK

80g char siu sauce (buy from an Asian supermarket)

2 garlic cloves, minced on a Microplane for best results

50g fresh root ginger, peeled and sliced

1 tbsp Chinese five-spice powder

1 tbsp ground white pepper

1 tbsp dark soy sauce

2 tbsp honey

900g piece well-trimmed pork shoulder (10–15cm in length and 5–7cm thick)

FOR THE GLAZE

2 tbsp char siu sauce

2 tbsp honey

FOR THE RICE

2 litres water

2 tbsp salt

200g–300g long grain rice, washed

FOR THE SPINACH

500g fresh spinach

10g butter

1 tsp minced garlic – for best results use a Microplane

1 tsp freshly grated root ginger

salt

SERVES 4–6

I really enjoy char siu – I love the stickiness. Pick up a nice piece of pork with some fat, so that it caramelises nicely, and keep brushing it with the glaze while you cook it. Simple but tasty.

Marinate the meat · Put 80g of the char siu sauce into a shallow dish with the garlic, sliced ginger, Chinese five-spice, white pepper, soy sauce and two tablespoons of the honey. Mix well and add the pork shoulder, turning until well coated. Cover and chill for at least 3 hours or up to 12 hours. The longer you can leave it, the better the flavour.

Cook the meat · Preheat the air fryer to 200°C (400°F). Make the glaze by mixing the char siu sauce in a bowl with the honey. Drain the pork from the marinade and put it in the air fryer, brushing over a little of the glaze. Cook for 15 minutes, brushing with the glaze every 3–4 minutes, until the pork is cooked through and tender with a lovely dark glaze. Transfer to a platter and cover loosely with tin foil, then set aside in a warm place to rest for 10–15 minutes.

Cook the rice · Meanwhile, put the water and salt in a large pan and bring to the boil. Add the rice, give one good stir, and cook for 12 minutes until just tender, then drain well and return to the pan. Cover with a lid to keep warm until needed.

Prepare the spinach · Wash the spinach well in a colander in the sink under cold running water and remove any tough stalks. Heat a large non-stick frying pan over a medium heat. Add the butter with the garlic and ginger and sauté for 2 minutes. Add the spinach, mixing quickly until it is all wilted down, then season with salt.

Time to serve · Carve the rested char siu pork into 2cm slices on the diagonal. Spoon the rice into warm bowls and arrange slices of the pork on top. Finish with the sautéed fragrant spinach.

ROASTED GARLIC CONFIT

6 large garlic bulbs, unpeeled
2 fresh thyme sprigs
2 fresh rosemary sprigs
100ml olive oil
sea salt flakes

MAKES ABOUT 400G JAR

This is something that works really well in the air fryer. Its intense heat cooks the garlic quickly and gives it a nice roast. You can use it for garlic butter or squeezed into a sauce or mayonnaise. It's perfect to chop down and add to anything, really, to give it that big natural roasted-garlic flavour.

Cook the garlic · Preheat the air fryer to 180°C (350°F). Take two squares of tin foil. Cut 1cm off the top of each garlic bulb and put three onto each piece of tin foil. Scatter over the thyme, rosemary and some salt and drizzle the oil on top. Wrap into two loose parcels and cook for 25 minutes, until the garlic is completely tender. Check by lightly squeezing – it should give easily.

Finish the confit · Keep the garlic confit in the parcel and store in a sealed container. Squeeze out the garlic confit as needed. This will keep for up to a week in the fridge.

FRIED CABBAGE WITH MISO MAYONNAISE

2 spring cabbages
60ml extra virgin olive oil
sea salt flakes
60ml miso mayonnaise (page 249)
2 tsp toasted sesame seeds

SERVES 2-4

The air fryer needs a little bit of oil or fat, so by squeezing the water out of the cabbage and rolling it extra virgin olive oil, the intense heat fries and chars the cabbage leaves perfectly and quickly. This is really simple, and with the miso mayo and toasted seeds, it tastes great.

Boil the cabbage · Bring a large pan of salted water to the boil. Strip off and discard the first layer of leaves from the cabbages, then add to the pan and cook for 5 minutes until completely soft. Check that a sharp knife will go in easily. Place the cabbages in cold water and leave for 3–4 minutes, then gently squeeze out the water. Cut each one in half and then gently squeeze out the water again, without crushing the cabbage.

Air fry the cabbage · Preheat the air fryer to 200°C (400°F). Roll the cabbage halves in the oil and season with salt, and then add to the air fryer. Cook for 10 minutes. Using a tongs, turn the cabbage over and cook for another 6 minutes. Turn the air fryer on to max crispiness and cook for another 3 minutes, until the cabbage is charred brown and evenly crispy.

Time to serve · Transfer the cabbage to warm plates and drizzle over the miso mayonnaise, then scatter over the toasted sesame seeds.

POLENTA CHIPS WITH LEMON AND PINK PEPPERCORN MAYONNAISE

1 litre chicken stock (make with 2 chicken stock jelly pots)

2 garlic cloves, peeled

4 fresh thyme sprigs, leaves removed and finely chopped

1 tbsp salt

250g instant polenta, plus extra 100g for coating

4 fresh rosemary sprigs, leaves stripped and finely chopped

½ tsp ground white pepper

100g freshly grated Parmesan, plus 1 tsp for garnish

100g butter

100ml milk

a little olive oil spray

FOR THE MAYONNAISE

50g lemon mayonnaise (page 247)

1 tbsp chopped fresh chives

½ tbsp chopped tarragon

2 tbsp crushed pink peppercorns

SERVES 6-8

This is a great alternative to potato chips. Using instant polenta means that it cooks so quickly. Kids love these.

Make the liquid infusion · Place the chicken stock in a heavy-based pan with the garlic, thyme and salt. Bring to the boil, then remove from the heat and leave to infuse for 10 minutes, then pass through a sieve into a jug.

Cook the polenta · Return the infused liquid to a low heat, then slowly pour in the polenta and cook on a low heat for 6–8 minutes. The texture should be like loose mashed potato.

Flavour the polenta · Remove the cooked polenta from the heat and beat in the rosemary, white pepper, Parmesan and butter. Line a 33cm × 40cm shallow baking tin with cling film and spray with oil. Then pour in the polenta mixture, smoothing down the top. Leave to cool, then spray the top with extra oil and cover with cling film. Chill in the fridge for at least 30 minutes, until set firm. This can be made up to a day before serving and kept in the fridge.

Make the polenta chips · Preheat the air fryer to 200°C (400°F). Spray the bottom of the basket with oil. Turn the set polenta out onto a chopping board, and cut into thick chips (each about 10cm in length and 3cm wide). Tip the polenta chips into the milk, then take them out, shaking off any excess, and roll in the rest of the polenta.

Cook the polenta chips · Arrange the chips in the air fryer basket and lightly spray on top with oil. Cook for 20 minutes, turn over with a spatula and cook for another 10 minutes, until crisp and golden brown.

Time to serve · Mix the herbs and peppercorn through the lemon mayonnaise, and sprinkle a teaspoon of Parmesan on top. Transfer the polenta chips to kitchen paper and season with salt. Arrange on a platter with a couple of spoonfuls of mayonnaise.

CRISPY PARMESAN COURGETTE WITH CHERRY TOMATOES AND BURRATA

100g panko breadcrumbs
2 eggs
50ml milk
50g plain flour
1 courgette
50g Parmesan
200g cherry tomatoes on the vine
extra virgin olive oil, for drizzling
about 100g basil pesto (page 218)
1 ball buffalo burrata
20ml balsamic vinegar
sea salt flakes
Parmesan shavings, basil leaves and rocket, to garnish

SERVES 1–2

All Mediterranean flavours here in this quick, convenient dish. It cooks with ease in the air fryer, and the fat in the cheese adds to the colour. It can be served as a starter or made a little bigger for a main course.

Prepare the courgette · Blitz half the panko breadcrumbs in a food processor until very fine, then put into a shallow dish with the rest of the breadcrumbs and stir well. Break the eggs into a separate shallow dish and whisk with the milk. Put the flour on to a tray. Using a mandolin, cut the courgettes into 2cm slices, then toss them in the flour, dip in the egg mixture and coat in the breadcrumbs. Put on a tray lined with parchment paper

Air fry the courgette · Heat the air fryer to 200°C (400°F). Line with parchment paper and, using a Microplane, add a generous grating of the Parmesan on the bottom. Add a single layer of the courgettes and another generous grating of the Parmesan on top, and season with flaky salt. Cook for 10 minutes, then turn the courgette slices over and grate over the rest of the Parmesan. Cook for another 4 minutes at max crisp. Put the cherry tomatoes into the air fryer for the last 2 minutes, dressed with a little olive oil and seasoned with salt.

Time to serve · Spoon two to three spoonfuls of the pesto on to the plate to make a round even base. Add the burrata, then arrange the courgettes and cherry tomatoes on the vine on top and pour over the balsamic vinegar. Season with salt and add a drizzle of extra virgin olive oil. Scatter over some Parmesan shavings and basil leaves, then add another drizzle of extra virgin olive oil and another of balsamic vinegar. Finish with some rocket leaves and some more pesto, if liked.

STICKY SOY-GLAZED CHICKEN

1 whole cornfed chicken
   (about 1.6–2kg)
1 litre water
1 red onion, peeled and
   quartered
30g piece fresh root ginger,
   sliced
3 star anise
150ml light soy sauce
140g dark brown sugar
1 tbsp honey

SERVES 4

I love cooking this because it's all in one pot, and then it glazes and cooks at the same time in the air fryer.

Prepare the chicken · Flip over the chicken so the backbone is facing you. Using a large knife or poultry shears, cut down either side of the backbone then discard. Turn the chicken over and cut the chicken in half.

Poach the chicken · Bring a large pan of water to the boil and add the chicken for 20 seconds to remove any impurities. Discard the water. Transfer the chicken to a plate. Put a litre of fresh water in a large pan with the red onion, ginger, star anise, soy sauce and sugar. Add the blanched chicken, making sure the pieces are fully immersed, and bring to a boil over a high heat. Reduce the heat to a simmer, then cover with a lid and cook gently for 30 minutes. Carefully lift out the chicken and pat off any excess liquid with kitchen paper.

Air fry the chicken · Preheat the air fryer to 180°C (350°F). Arrange the poached chicken halves in the air fryer and cook for 15 minutes.

Make the glaze · Meanwhile, strain 300ml of the cooking liquid into a clean pan and add the honey, then simmer over a medium heat, reducing until it's syrupy – but not burnt. This will take about 10–15 minutes.

Finish the chicken · Increase the heat on the air fryer to max crisp, and cook the pieces of chicken for another 8 minutes, until the skin is nice and crispy. Arrange on warm plates and brush with the glaze before serving.

SIMPLE

SUPPERS

Keeping it simple can be a challenge, but here are some supper ideas that hopefully will inspire you to try new versions of some familiar dishes. All these recipes can be served with some of the Side Cars (pages 168–182), depending on how much time you have. Whether it's midweek with the kids or a weekend date night, once you get all your ingredients together and read the recipe twice, so you can be really organised, you'll be good to go! If you don't have the jars mentioned in the recipes, feel free to swap them out for what is handy.

BATTERED COD WITH PEAS, MINT AND CURRIED CRÈME FRAICHE

FOR THE CURRIED CRÈME FRAICHE
50ml olive oil
½ onion, diced
2 garlic cloves, thinly sliced (on a mandolin)
12g mild Madras curry powder
50g crème fraiche (chilled)
zest of ½ lemon

FOR THE LEMON GARNISH
1 lemon, halved

FOR THE FISH
vegetable oil, for deep-frying
500–600g piece of boneless and skinless cod fillet
25g plain flour, for dusting
1 quantity beer and vodka batter (page 223)

FOR THE PEAS
100g frozen peas
50ml water
2 tsp softened butter
8 fresh mint leaves, thinly sliced
pinch of sugar

sea salt flakes and freshly ground black pepper

SERVES 2

Thanks to Heston Blumenthal, the chef world loves this style of batter, but I think dads can do this too. Don't worry about the alcohol – it cooks out, but the result is super light and the texture is so delicate and crunchy. Throw spoonfuls of it in on top of your fish in the fryer for the best results.

Make the curried crème fraiche · Heat the olive oil in a frying pan over a medium heat and sauté the onion and garlic for 3–4 minutes, until softened and transparent. Stir in the curry powder and cook for 2 minutes, stirring. Leave to cool, then transfer to a chopping board and chop finely with a sharp knife. Transfer to a bowl and mix in the crème fraiche and lemon zest. Cover with cling film and chill until needed.

Prepare the lemon garnish · Heat a heavy-based frying pan over a low heat. Add the lemon, then cook, with no oil, cut-side down for 6–7 minutes, until well coloured and caramelised. Set aside.

Cook the fish · Preheat a deep-fat fryer to 160°C (320°F) with vegetable oil – no higher or it will blow the batter off the fish. Cut the cod into two even-sized pieces and dry with kitchen paper. Season the cod and toss in the flour, shaking off any excess, and then dip in the batter. Carefully lower each piece into the hot oil and then quickly add a few more spoonfuls of the batter on top. This helps to make a lighter, better crust on top of the fish. Fry for 6–8 minutes, depending on the thickness of the fish, until crisp and golden. Using a large slotted spoon, lift the fish out and drain on kitchen paper. Season with salt.

Make the peas · Put the peas and water in a small pan with the butter and bring to a simmer over a medium heat, then cook for a minute until warmed through. Fold in the mint and sugar. Keep warm.

Time to serve · Spoon the chilled curried crème fraiche on to warm plates, then add some peas. Add the deep-fried cod and season with salt flakes. Garnish each one with a piece of burnt lemon.

SHEPHERD'S PIE WITH PARMESAN MASH

80g olive oil

800g lamb mince

2 carrots, grated

3 garlic cloves, grated

1 large onion, grated

1 leek, finely chopped (white part only)

2 celery sticks, trimmed and grated

2 tbsp tomato purée

300ml red wine

700ml chicken stock (from a cube is fine)

1 large sprig of rosemary

2 large sprigs of thyme

1 tbsp prepared English mustard

2 tsp Worcestershire sauce

1kg large baking potatoes (such as Rooster)

1 egg yolk

70g freshly grated Parmesan

100g butter

100g milk

salt and freshly ground white pepper

SERVES 6-8

A staple nourishing classic, perfect on a winter's evening. I've added a little bit of Parmesan into the mash, which gives an extra layer of moreishness. Serve with some triple-cooked chips (page 174) or one of the salads in this book on the side.

Sauté the mince · Heat a shallow casserole dish over a medium heat. Add a couple of tablespoons of the oil and sauté half the lamb mince for about 10 minutes, until it is golden brown with good caramelisation. Tip into a bowl, then do the same thing with the other half.

Cook the vegetables · Add another couple of tablespoons of oil to the same pan, then sauté the carrots and garlic for about 5 minutes, until they start to colour – this will happen quicker than normal, as you'll still have all the lamb flavour in the bottom of the pan. Add the onion, leek and celery and continue to sauté for 6–8 minutes, until all the vegetables are tender and nicely coloured.

Finish the sauce · Add the tomato purée to the cooked vegetables and cook for 1 minute, stirring. Pour in the wine and allow it to bubble down, scraping up and stirring in any sediment from the bottom of the pan. Add the chicken stock, herbs, mustard and Worcestershire sauce, then add back in the drained lamb mince and season with salt and pepper. Bring to a simmer, then reduce the heat and simmer gently for 1 hour, until the lamb is meltingly tender and the sauce has nicely reduced. Remove the thyme and rosemary sprigs.

Cook the potatoes · Meanwhile, preheat the oven to 180°C (350°F/Gas Mark 4). Pierce the potatoes a few times to prevent them from bursting, then bake directly on the oven shelf for 1 hour, until soft when gently squeezed.

Mash the potatoes · Remove the potatoes from the oven and cut in half, then, using a spoon, scoop the flesh out into a bowl. Mash with a potato ricer or Mouli and weigh the results – you'll need 600g in total. Season with salt and pepper, then beat in the egg yolk, 50g Parmesan, butter and milk.

Cook the pie · Spoon or pipe the mashed potatoes over the lamb mince and score with a fork. Sprinkle the remaining Parmesan on top, the clean the edges of the dish and bake for about 45 minutes, until bubbling and golden brown.

Time to serve · Put the casserole dish of shepherd's pie in the middle of the table so that everyone can help themselves.

BAKED SAUSAGE BOULANGÈRE

500ml chicken stock (made
  with 1 chicken jelly stock
  pot)
3 garlic cloves, peeled
3 fresh thyme sprigs
3 bay leaves
4 large baking potatoes, peeled
  (Maris Pipers, 900g–1kg)
3 fresh rosemary sprigs
4 large Toulouse sausages (or
  a good-quality pork sausage
  from your butcher)
200g caramelised onion
  marmalade (page 234)
100g butter, diced
salt and freshly ground white
  pepper

SERVES 4

This is one of my favourite dishes from my training in French kitchens.
I've used Toulouse sausage here, but you can use whatever ones you
can get your hands on – I recommend good thick pork sausages from
the butcher. Get your onion cooked beforehand and into the jar so that
it's ready. Don't slice your potatoes too thin – for better flavour, you
need them thick enough to drink all of the stock.

Prepare the herb potatoes · Preheat the oven to 180°C (350°F/Gas Mark
4). Put the chicken stock in a pan with the garlic, half of the thyme and the
bay leaves, then bring to the boil. Meanwhile, cut the potatoes on a mandolin
(about ½ cm) and place them in a baking tin. Pour over the boiling stock
mixture and bake for 8–10 minutes, until just tender but still holding their
shape. Remove from the oven and set aside to cool down a little, reserving
the stock.

Make the herb seasoning · Pick the rest of the thyme and the rosemary
leaves off the stalks and finely chop with a large knife. Set aside until needed.

Cook the sausages · In a non-stick frying pan over a medium heat, sauté
the sausages for a few minutes until sealed on the outside but still raw in the
middle. Cut into 1cm slices and set aside.

Heat the caramelised onions · Put the caramelised onion marmalade into a
pan and reheat gently, stirring occasionally.

Layer up and bake the dish · Rub about a quarter of the butter into the
bottom of a round ovenproof dish and arrange an overlapping layer of the
potatoes on it – about a third of them. Add a spoonful of the stock and a few
pieces of butter. Season with salt and pepper, then add half of the caramelised
onion marmalade and put half of the sliced sausage on top. Add a little more
stock followed by another layer of potato. Season again and add the rest of the
marmalade and the sausage as before, then finish with a layer of the potato,
the last few pieces of butter and a little more stock. Sprinkle over the herb
seasoning. Bake for 30–40 minutes, until the sausages are cooked through, the
potatoes have absorbed most of the stock, and a nice crust has formed.

Time to serve · Bring the dish of sausage boulangère straight to the table so
everyone can help themselves.

CHARGRILLED CHICKEN CIABATTA SANDWICH

1 skinless and boneless large
   chicken breast
olive oil, for cooking
3 slices rindless smoked
   streaky bacon
1 ciabatta
about 2 tbsp basil pesto (page
   218)
about 2 tbsp lemon
   mayonnaise (page 247)
2 ripe avocadoes, halved,
   stones removed and thinly
   sliced
2–3 thin slices smoked
   Cheddar cheese (Applewood)
1 ripe large tomato, cut into
   slices
1 Little Gem lettuce
2 tsp lemon, garlic and
   tarragon dressing (page 243)
a few fresh basil leaves
handful watercress sprigs, plus
   extra to garnish
sea salt and freshly ground
   black pepper
triple-cooked chips, to serve
   (page 174)

SERVES 2

Just a good, honest chicken sandwich here. The lemon mayo makes it a little fresher, and the sliced avocado works great with the pesto.

Cook the meat · Heat a griddle pan over a high heat. Cut through the chicken lengthways, with your knife parallel to the cutting board, into two scallops and then drizzle with olive oil and season. Add to the heated griddle and cook for 1–2 minutes on each side until cooked through and nicely charred. Transfer to a plate, then add the bacon to the pan and season with pepper. Cook for a minute or so on each side until crisp.

Prepare the bread · Meanwhile, preheat the grill to high. Cut the ciabatta loaf in half and arrange cut-side up on the grill rack. Toast for a couple of minutes until lightly golden. Spread the bottom half with the pesto and the top half with the lemon mayonnaise.

Make the sandwich · Cover the pesto side with the avocado and add the smoked bacon, then cover with the cheese. Put it back under the grill until the cheese has melted. Meanwhile, put the tomato on the lemon mayonnaise side and cover with the chargrilled chicken. Discard the outer leaves from the Little Gem, break it into a bowl and lightly coat in the lemon, garlic and tarragon dressing, then pile it on the chicken with the basil leaves. Scatter the watercress over the melted cheese.

Time to serve · Sandwich together both layered-up pieces of the ciabatta and press down gently, then cut in half and arrange on plates with the triple-cooked chips.

TOMAHAWK STEAK WITH ONION RINGS AND CHIMICHURRI

1 tomahawk (or a double rib eye) steak
2 tbsp olive oil
vegetable oil, for deep-frying
1 large onion
120g Rice Krispies
120g instant mashed potato
200g plain flour
4 tsp smoked paprika
3 tsp garlic powder
6 tsp curry powder, plus extra for seasoning
1 quantity tempura batter (page 222)
1 quantity fresh herb green chimichurri sauce (page 221)
salt and freshly ground black pepper
triple-cooked chips, to serve (see page 174)

SERVES 2-3

You can just use a good piece of rib eye from your butcher if you can't find one with the bone. Try and get something dry aged if you can. These onion rings are a little different but taste really good with the Rice Krispies and dried potato, which adds an extra layer of crunchiness. No sticky sauces here: I've just used a fresh herb chimichurri with a little chilli that can be served at room temperature – nice and fresh and summery.

Prepare the steak · Preheat the oven to 170°C (325°F/Gas Mark 3). Heat an ovenproof frying pan, large enough to fit the steak, over a high heat. Season the steak all over. Add the olive oil to the pan and then sear the steak on all sides to achieve a good dark-brown crust. Place in the oven and cook for 10 minutes per 500g for rare. If you have a thermometer, you can check this – the inside temperature should be 55°C (130°F), 60°C (140°F) for medium rare, 65°C (150°F) for medium well and 70°C (160°F) for well done. Remove from the oven and cover loosely with tin foil. Leave to rest for 15–20 minutes.

Make the onion rings · Meanwhile, preheat the deep-fat fryer to 170°C (325°F). Peel the onion and cut into 1cm slices, then separate into rings and place in a bowl of cold water to soak for 30 minutes. In a food processor, pulse the Rice Krispies to a thick crumb. Put the Rice Krispies and instant mashed potato in a bowl and mix. Put the flour and the spices in a separate bowl and mix well. Drain the onion rings and then remove the transparent skin membrane. Working in small batches, toss the onion rings in the spiced flour mixture and coat in the tempura batter, then toss in the Rice Krispie mixture. Deep-fry for 2–3 minutes until crisp and golden brown. Remove with a slotted spoon and drain on kitchen paper and season with salt and curry powder. Keep warm in a low oven.

Time to serve · Place the rested tomahawk on a chopping board and drizzle over the green chimichurri. Add a large pile of the onion rings to the side and a bowl of the triple-cooked chips.

THE DADDY BURGER

680g minced beef (10% fat)

sunflower or vegetable oil, for deep-frying

1 onion

100g plain flour

2 eggs, beaten

200g breadcrumbs

4 burger buns (page 207)

240g tomato and yellow pepper relish (page 242)

240g caramelised onion marmalade (page 234)

4 crisp butterhead lettuce leaves

1 tomato, thinly sliced

4 slices smoked Cheddar cheese (Applewood)

salt and freshly ground black pepper

SERVES 4

There are two jars in this recipe, the relish and the marmalade, but if you go to the effort of making them, they can be stored for weeks. Get the best mince you can from your butcher, and serve this burger as a treat with some of our triple-cooked chips.

Make the beef patties · Heat a griddle pan until smoking hot. Put the minced beef into a bowl and season with salt and pepper, then divide into four and, using your hands or a burger press, shape into patties about the thickness of the top of your thumb. Add to the griddle and cook on each side until medium (2–3 minutes per side) then turn off the heat and leave them to rest until you are ready for them.

Make the onion rings · Meanwhile, preheat the deep-fat fryer to 160°C (320°F). Peel the onion and cut into 1cm slices, then separate into rings and place in a bowl of cold water to soak for 30 minutes. Drain the onion rings, remove the transparent skin membrane so that the batter sticks better, then toss them in the flour. Coat them in the beaten egg, and then toss them in the breadcrumbs. Deep-fry for 2–3 minutes, until crisp and golden brown. Remove with a slotted spoon and drain on kitchen paper, then season with salt. Keep warm in a low oven.

Assemble the burgers · Preheat the grill to hot. Split the burger buns and toast for a minute or two until lightly golden. Add a dollop of the tomato and yellow pepper relish to the bottom halves with a spoonful of the caramelised onion marmalade, the lettuce and tomato slices. Add a beef patty, cover with the cheese and flash under the grill again to melt. Finish each one with a large crispy onion ring. Add the rest of the caramelised onion marmalade and tomato and yellow pepper relish to the burger-bun tops and then put them on top of the burgers.

Time to serve · Put the burgers on warm serving plates with the triple-cooked chips and serve a separate bowl with the rest of the crispy onion rings.

CRISPY COD BURGER WITH PICKLED CUCUMBER AND GOCHUJANG MAYONNAISE

vegetable oil, for deep-frying

25g plain flour

2 × 150g boneless and skinless cod fillets

375ml tempura batter (page 222)

sea salt flakes, for seasoning

½ lemon

2 burger buns, split in half (page 207)

2 little baby Gem lettuce leaves, thinly sliced

FOR THE PICKLED CUCUMBER

2 cucumbers

300ml water

100ml white wine vinegar

100g caster sugar

3 garlic cloves, peeled

1 fresh thyme sprig

100ml extra virgin olive oil

8 fresh dill sprigs, fronds removed

FOR THE MAYONNAISE

60g egg yolks

15g Dijon mustard

15g sherry vinegar

12g dark soy sauce

juice of 2 limes, plus finely grated zest of 1 lime

40g gochujang paste (buy in an Asian supermarket)

18g honey

160ml vegetable oil

60g extra virgin olive oil

SERVES 2

If you don't have time to make your own burger buns here, just get them from the shop. The heat and the cooling of the gochujang mayo and the pickled cucumber are a nice addition to the cod. They'll be coming back for more.

Make the pickled cucumber · Peel the cucumbers with a speed peeler. Put the water in a pan with the vinegar, sugar, garlic and thyme. Bring to the boil, then stir in the olive oil and leave to cool down. Put the cucumber and dill in a suitable container and pour over the warm pickling mixture, making sure that it covers the cucumber completely. Leave for at least 1 hour at room temperature or up to 1 week if secured with a lid and stored in the fridge.

Make the mayonnaise · Put the egg yolks in a bowl with the mustard, sherry vinegar, soy sauce, lime juice, gochujang and honey. Pour both oils into a jug. Whisk the ingredients together in the bowl and then gradually whisk in the oil mixture, drop by drop, until you have a thick mayonnaise. Stir in the lime zest, then transfer to a small bowl and cover with cling film or put in a squeezy bottle. Chill until needed. This will last up to 1 week in the fridge.

Cook the cod · Preheat the oven to 180°C (350°F/Gas Mark 4) and a deep-fat fryer to 160°C (320°F). Put the flour on a plate and use it to lightly dust the cod, shaking off any excess. Dip the cod in the batter, and if you have a squeezy bottle put some of the batter into it. Add the coated cod to the hot oil and, using a spoon or squeezy bottle, add some more batter on top to give a nice crisp golden texture. Cook for 3–4 minutes, then drain on kitchen paper, transfer to the oven on a baking sheet and finish cooking for 2 minutes. Season with salt and a squeeze of lemon juice.

Build the burger · Preheat the grill to medium. Toast the burger buns until lightly golden. Spread a tablespoon of the mayonnaise on the bottom, cover with lettuce leaves and then top with some drained pickled cucumber. Add a piece of crispy cod and then add another tablespoon of the mayonnaise. Finish with the tops of the buns.

Time to serve · Arrange the cod burgers on warm plates with the triple-cooked chips and some of the extra mayonnaise in a small dish for dipping.

PASTA

What families don't love pasta?
Here I've chosen some familiar pasta recipes
that, done right, can be quick and still delicious
– with a little technique, you can bring out the
best flavour. All of them can be made with dried
pasta for your convenience. I've tried to stay as
authentic to the dishes as I can, but I have thrown
a few cheats into the mix. These are some of my
favourite plates when craving cheese
and a bit of richness.

CACIO E PEPE LINGUINE

4 tsp salt
150g linguine
30g freshly grated Parmesan,
  plus extra for garnishing
30g freshly grated pecorino
1½ tbsp crème fraiche
knob of butter
1 tsp freshly ground black
  pepper

SERVES 2

Such a simple pasta dish but one of my favourites – the toasted black pepper and the pecorino cheese go great together. Here I use a blender to get a super-smooth sauce. Serve this on a warm plate and eat immediately.

Cook the pasta · Put 3 teaspoons of the salt into a large pan of boiling water and return to a rolling boil. Add the linguine and cook following the packet instructions. Reserve 40ml of the cooking water and then drain into a colander in the sink. Refresh under cold running water.

Make the sauce · Put the reserved cooking water into a Nutribullet or blender and add the Parmesan, pecorino and crème fraiche with the remaining teaspoon of salt. Blend until smooth.

Finish the dish · Heat a large non-stick frying pan over a low heat. Melt the butter and add the black pepper, then toast for a few seconds. Remove from the heat and toss with the drained linguine and sauce, until everything is well mixed and just warmed through. The heat of the pan will bring the sauce together.

Time to serve · Divide the cacio e pepe among warm plates and garnish with extra Parmesan.

LINGUINE CARBONARA

1 tbsp salt

300g linguine

30g guanciale or pancetta, cut into lardons

1 garlic clove, peeled

2 large eggs plus 2 yolks

50g freshly grated Parmesan, plus extra for garnish

50g freshly grated pecorino

3 heaped tbsp crème fraiche, plus a little extra if needed

1 tbsp freshly ground black pepper

juice of 1 lemon

SERVES 4

Another classic. If you can't get the guanciale you can use smoked bacon or smoked pancetta. I've cheated a little here and stabilised the sauce with a spoonful of crème fraiche, which also adds great flavour – and if this upsets any Italians, forgive me, but I have one word for you: 'Schillaci'.

Cook the pasta · Bring a large pan of water to the boil with the salt. Swirl in the linguine and cook for about 8 minutes until 'al dente'.

Cook the bacon · Meanwhile, heat a non-stick frying pan over a medium heat. Add the guanciale or pancetta lardons and cook for a couple of minutes until it has begun to crisp up and release its fat. Then, using a Microplane or other fine grater, grate in the garlic and continue to sauté for another 20–30 seconds.

Mix the sauce · Put the eggs and yolks into a Nutribullet or blender with the Parmesan, pecorino, crème fraiche and pepper. Blitz the sauce until smooth.

Finish the dish · Reserve a cup of the cooking water, then quickly drain the linguine in a colander in the sink. Return the cooked linguine to the pan with the sizzling guanciale and garlic, then add the lemon juice and three ladlefuls of the reserved pasta water. Bring to a simmer, and when the pasta is steaming hot remove from the heat. (It's very important that it's off the heat so the eggs don't cook.) Then quickly fold in the egg mixture until you have a smooth, silky sauce, adding a little more crème fraiche or pasta water if necessary.

Time to serve · Divide the linguine carbonara among warm plates and garnish with extra Parmesan to serve.

SPAGHETTI MEATBALLS BOLOGNESE-STYLE

700g minced beef
1 tsp dried oregano
1 tsp herbes de Provence
½ tsp harissa powder
½ tsp onion powder
50ml olive oil, plus a little
    extra
350g mushrooms, trimmed
    and sliced
8 garlic cloves, thinly sliced
    (on a mandolin)
1 large onion, diced
3 fresh sprigs of thyme, leaves
    stripped off
3 bay leaves
2 tsp tomato purée
2 × 400g tins chopped
    tomatoes
4 ripe tomatoes, quartered and
    deseeded
500ml water
300g spaghetti
salt and freshly ground black
    pepper
freshly grated Parmesan, extra
    virgin olive oil and fresh
    basil leaves, to garnish

SERVES 4-6

This is an old favourite that kids love. Give the meatballs as much colour as you can in the pan, then get them back into the sauce to cook slowly. I like to do the garlic *Goodfellas* style – slicing it as thin as I can on the mandolin, then cooking it till soft in the oil.

Prepare the meatballs · Mix the minced beef, herbs and spices in a bowl and season with four teaspoons of salt and plenty of pepper. Using slightly wetted hands, shape into 40g balls. Heat a sauté pan over a medium heat. Add about two tablespoons of the oil and sauté the meatballs for 5–6 minutes, until golden brown all over – you may have to do this in batches, depending on the size of your pan; if you want nice colourisation, it's important not to crowd the meatballs. Transfer to a plate and set aside.

Cook the Bolognese · Pulse the mushrooms in a food processor until finely chopped. Heat the remaining olive oil in a sauté pan over a high heat. Add the garlic and cook for a few minutes to soften. Add the mushrooms and sauté to colour. Turn down the heat and stir in the onion, thyme and bay leaves, then cover with a lid and cook for about 10 minutes, until the onions have softened and are transparent. Stir in the tomato purée and cook for a few minutes, stirring. Add the tinned and fresh tomatoes and 2 teaspoons of salt and stir well to combine. Once bubbling, stir in the water.

Finish the dish · Add the meatballs back into the sauce, then cover and simmer gently for 1 hour and 15 minutes. Remove the lid and check the sauce has thickened nicely – you can simmer it down for another 15 minutes if you think it needs it. If it gets too dry, add a little more water.

Cook the spaghetti · Meanwhile, bring a large pan of salted water to the boil. Swirl in the spaghetti and cook for 8–10 minutes, or according to packet instructions, until 'al dente'. Drain the pasta into a colander in the sink and toss in a little more olive oil.

Time to serve · Divide the spaghetti among bowls and spoon the meatballs with the sauce on top, then scatter over the Parmesan and drizzle with a little extra virgin olive oil. Garnish with the basil leaves.

PORK PAPPARDELLE WITH PUMPKIN AND SAGE

200ml olive oil, plus 3–4 tbsp for the pappardelle

400g piece of pumpkin, peeled and diced

3 fresh rosemary sprigs, 1 whole and 2 with leaves stripped and finely chopped

120g butter

2 tsp honey

160ml cream

juice of ½ lemon

1 small onion, diced

2 garlic cloves, thinly sliced

280g pork mince

2 fresh thyme sprigs, leaves stripped

300g egg pappardelle

vegetable or sunflower oil, for frying

2 fresh sage sprigs

2 tsp crème fraiche

salt and freshly ground black pepper

freshly grated Parmesan and extra virgin olive oil, to serve

SERVES 4

Kitchen Note: You can garnish this pasta dish with some roasted pork belly (see page 136). Simply cut the cooked pork belly into 3cm chunks and fry it in a hot ovenproof frying pan to crisp up, then finish it in a preheated oven at 180°C (350°F/Gas Mark 4) for 10 minutes, until very crisp and golden brown. Drain on kitchen paper and add it to the plate at the end.

This can be a starter or a main course – if you want a bigger portion, just add more pork. The rosemary, pumpkin, sage and Parmesan go really well together. If you can master this, you'll cook this dish again and again.

Cook the pumpkin sauce · Heat a sauté pan over a medium heat and add 100ml of the olive oil. Tip in the pumpkin and the rosemary sprig that has been left whole and sauté for 8–10 minutes, until coloured. Add half of the butter, tossing until melted. Add the honey and cream and bring to the boil. Transfer to a blender, then add the lemon juice and blend until smooth. Set aside.

Prepare the meatballs · Heat a sauté pan over a medium heat. Add another splash of olive oil and the rest of the butter, then sauté the onion and garlic for about 10 minutes, until softened and transparent. Transfer to a bowl and, once cool, mix with the pork mince, thyme and the finely chopped rosemary and season generously. Roll the mixture into 10g balls. Heat the rest of the olive oil in a sauté pan over a medium heat. Sauté the meatballs in batches for 3–4 minutes, until cooked and golden brown all over. Transfer to a plate and set aside.

Cook the pappardelle · Meanwhile, bring a large pan of salted water to the boil. Add the pappardelle and cook for 3–4 minutes or according to packet instructions until 'al dente'. Take 100ml of the cooking water in a cup, then drain the pasta into a colander in the sink and quickly refresh under cold running water, and then toss the pasta in 3 or 4 tablespoons of olive oil.

Fry the sage · Heat some vegetable or sunflower oil in a small pan. Pick the sage leaves and fry for 3 minutes, then tip on to kitchen paper to drain. Leave to crisp up.

Finish the dish · Put a clean sauté pan back on a medium heat and add the pumpkin sauce and meatballs and simmer for a few minutes, stirring. Then fold in the pasta with the crème fraiche until everything is nicely warmed through. Season to taste.

Time to serve · Divide the pork pappardelle with pumpkin among wide rimmed bowls and garnish with the Parmesan. Add some crispy sage and a drizzle of extra virgin olive oil with some crispy roast pork belly, if liked – see kitchen note.

WARM PASTA SALAD WITH SPRING VEG, WHIPPED RICOTTA AND HERBS

4 dried or fresh lasagne sheets
1 tbsp extra virgin olive oil
12 tbsp/180ml lemon, garlic and tarragon dressing (see page 243)
1 bunch fine asparagus, trimmed
200g frozen peas
200g frozen broad beans
80g mascarpone
80g ricotta
juice and zest of 1 lemon
20g fresh mint
20g fresh tarragon
20g fresh chives
salt and freshly ground white pepper

SERVES 4

Serve this dish just warm. The lemon, garlic and tarragon dressing adds a nice acidity to the flavours and cuts through the cheese. This is great coming into spring and perfect for the vegetarians in your family.

Cook the lasagne sheets · Bring a large pan of salted water to the boil. Rub the lasagne sheets with the oil to prevent them from sticking, then cook for 4–5 minutes or according to the packet instructions until 'al dente'. Drain into a colander in the sink and quickly refresh under cold running water. Set aside on a tray and brush with 4 tablespoons of lemon, garlic and tarragon dressing.

Blanch the vegetables · Bring a pan of salted water to the boil and blanch the asparagus for 2 minutes, then remove with a large slotted spoon and put in the colander. Again, quickly refresh to prevent further cooking. Add the peas and broad beans to the same pan and cook them for 1 minute, draining and refreshing as you did for the asparagus. Pinch the broad beans and slip them out of their skins.

Make the whipped ricotta · Put the mascarpone and ricotta in a food processor with the lemon juice and zest and pulse until whipped. (You can also use a whisk if you don't have a food processor.) Season to taste.

Heat the vegetables · Preheat the oven to 170°C (325°F/Gas Mark 3). Put all the vegetables in a baking tin and toss with 6 tablespoons of the dressing. Season with salt and pepper. Roast for 2 minutes until just warm.

Make the herb salad · Meanwhile, pick the mint and tarragon leaves off the stems and chop the chives into 2cm pieces. Gently toss together, then dress in enough of the lemon, garlic and tarragon dressing to lightly coat (about 2 tablespoons), then season to taste.

Time to serve · Spread the whipped ricotta on plates and top each one with a lasagne sheet. You can also assemble it all on a large platter. Scatter over the vegetables and finish with the herbs.

MAC AND CHEESE

425g béchamel sauce (see page 217)
2 bay leaves
100ml cream
50g red Cheddar, finely grated
40g freshly grated Parmesan
½ tsp grated nutmeg
300g macaroni
140g buffalo mozzarella ball, chopped
10g butter
8 fresh thyme sprigs
8 fresh rosemary sprigs
salt and freshly ground white pepper

SERVES 4-6

Who doesn't love this? So much creamy, cheesy indulgence here. All three cheeses play an important part: the mozzarella brings that stringy richness, the Cheddar gives great flavour, and the Parmesan makes the perfect crust.

Flavour the sauce · Put the béchamel sauce into a pan with the bay leaves and cream and cook over a low heat until warmed through, stirring to ensure it does not catch on the bottom. Remove from the heat and stir in the Cheddar and half of the Parmesan, then whisk until smooth. Add the nutmeg and season to taste, then remove the bay leaves.

Cook the pasta · Preheat the oven to 180°C (350°F/Gas Mark 4). Put a good pinch of salt into a large pan of boiling water and return to a rolling boil. Add the pasta and cook for 4 minutes, then drain.

Make the macaroni cheese · Fold the macaroni into the cheese sauce. Butter a large ovenproof dish, or four individual dishes, and fill with half of the macaroni mixture. Add a layer of mozzarella and sprinkle with half of the remaining Parmesan, then repeat the macaroni and mozzarella layers and bake for 20–30 minutes until bubbling and golden. Strip the thyme and rosemary leaves off the stalks and finely chop, then sprinkle over the remaining Parmesan. Flash under a hot grill for 2–3 minutes until it develops a golden crust.

PIZZA

Homemade pizza can be great, and I've included two pieces of equipment on page 115 that can take yours to the next level. There are recipes here for three doughs that I like: a classic thicker crust, a thin-crust smaller pizza – pizzetta – for the kids , and a quick and easy dough. The marriages of flavour in the toppings work really well, but once you get the dough done you can pretty much put what you like on top. It's great fun to get the kids involved in this on a Saturday afternoon!

GOOD THICK CRUST PIZZA DOUGH

FOR THE PREFERMENTED POOLISH
300ml cold water
3g dried yeast
300g Tipo '00' flour

FOR THE PIZZA DOUGH
1 quantity of the prefermented poolish
340ml cold water
700g Tipo '00' flour, plus extra for dusting
25g salt
10g extra virgin olive oil

MAKES 8-10 C. 200G DOUGH BALLS

This recipe is for a more authentic dough. You'll need to work a day or two ahead to get this dough ready to bake, but it's mostly hands-off time fermenting and proving. Once it's in the fridge in 200g balls, you can leave it for a day or so, which will make it easier to shape. You need to do a bit of playing around to get the technique that suits you, but what's better than fresh pizza?

Make the poolish · Pour the cold water into a rigid square container and add the yeast and flour, then, using your hand, mix until the dough comes together. Cover with cling film and make a few holes in it so that the mixture can breathe. Chill for 12 hours. After this time, it can be used to make pizza dough.

Make the pizza dough · Put the fermented poolish and water in a stand mixer with a dough hook and mix for 5 minutes. Tip in the flour and mix again for 5 minutes, until the dough has achieved a homogeneous texture. Add the salt and mix again for a couple of minutes, then add the olive oil. Mix for another 5 minutes until the dough comes together.

Prove the pizza dough · Remove the dough from the mixer and divide into 8–10 c. 200g balls. Leave them on a floured tray under a wet tea towel in a warm kitchen for at least 1.5–2 hours. The balls are then ready to use, or you can keep them in the fridge for a day or so, which will make them easier to shape.

THIN AND CRISPY PIZZA DOUGH (PIZZETTA)

500g Tipo '00' flour, plus extra
    for dusting
250ml warm water
6g dried yeast
5g salt
a little olive oil

**MAKES 4 C. 200G
DOUGH BALLS**

Roll this out thinly with a rolling pin and it will cook very quickly. Perfect for making little pizzas – pizzetta – with the kids.

Make the dough · Place the flour in a stand mixer with a dough hook. Mix the yeast and warm water together in a bowl to dissolve and then add to the flour. Mix for 10 minutes, then transfer to an oiled bowl. Cover with cling film and leave to rise in a warm place for 2 hours until it has doubled in size.

Finish the dough · Tip the risen dough back on to a lightly floured work surface and knead again for 3 minutes until you have a smooth dough. Return the dough to a clean oiled bowl and leave to rise again for 30 minutes.

Time to make pizza · When ready to make the pizzas, divide into 3 pieces, and shape into balls.

QUICK AND EASY PIZZA DOUGH

12g dried yeast
240ml warm water
1 tbsp olive oil
300g Tipo '00' flour, plus extra
    for dusting
12g granulated sugar
5g salt

**MAKES 3 C. 200G
DOUGH BALLS**

If time is an issue, here's a really quick pizza dough recipe I make at home that can be used instantly.

Make the dough · Mix the yeast and warm water together in a bowl to dissolve and then add the oil. In a separate bowl, mix the flour, sugar and salt. Make a hole in the dry mixture, and pour in the water and yeast, and mix with your hand until it comes together. It will be slightly sticky.

Finish the dough · Tip the dough on to a lightly floured work surface and knead for 5 minutes, until you have a smooth dough.

Time to make pizza · When ready to make the pizzas, divide into 3 pieces and shape into balls.

PROSCIUTTO AND MOZZARELLA PIZZA

200g pizza dough ball (see pages 110–112)

Tipo '00' flour, for dusting

about 4 tbsp pizza tomato sauce (page 224)

1 buffalo mozzarella ball (250g)

extra virgin olive oil, for drizzling

2 slices prosciutto ham

a few fresh basil leaves

small handful Parmesan shavings

sea salt and freshly ground black pepper

SERVES 1

Classic flavours these. The tomato sauce recipe is relatively quick, and cooked with the mozzarella on the pizza, with the ham and basil going on when it comes out of the oven. Don't forget to be generous with the salt and black pepper.

Get the dough ready · For the thick-crust dough, take it out of the fridge three hours before using. If you want air pockets and a light crispy base, don't use a rolling pin, as it flattens and pops the air bubbles (two days in the fridge will produce the most air bubbles).

Heat the oven of choice · To cook the pizzas, an Ooni pizza oven is best for controlling the temperature and a more authentic, smoky flavour. But you can also use a domestic oven preheated to 240°C (475°F/Gas Mark 9) along with a pizza steel (see below).

Shape the dough · When the thick-crust dough is at room temperature, you can use your fingers to gently stretch it out. Once it is about 16cm, place the disc over the tops of your hands (not palm side) and use them to stretch it further, up to about 25cm – the size of a large dinner plate. Take the same approach for the quick and easy dough. For the thin dough, roll it out as thin as you can to about 25cm.

Prepare the pizza base · If you are using a domestic oven, I recommend using a preheated pizza steel. This will ensure a crispy base. To slide the pizza on to a hot surface such as a pizza steel or an Ooni, you will need a paddle (also called a peel). If you don't have a pizza steel or an Ooni, you can build the pizza on a baking tray.

Make the pizza · Spread the pizza tomato sauce over the base in a thin, even layer, leaving a 2cm border around the edges to create the crust. Tear or slice the mozzarella and scatter on top. Give a light drizzle of olive oil and slide into the hot oven, turning the pizza halfway through if you are using an Ooni. In an Ooni on low heat, the pizza should be cooked in 4–6 minutes. In the oven, it should take about 10–12 minutes, depending on how thin or thick the dough is.

Time to serve · Remove the pizza from the oven and slide it on to a dinner plate, then, using a pizza wheel or scissors, cut into slices. Tear the prosciutto into strips and drape on top. Scatter over the basil, then give a drizzle of olive oil and finish with Parmesan shavings and plenty of salt and pepper.

DOUBLE CHEESE, DOUBLE MEAT PIZZA

200g pizza dough ball (see pages 110–112)

Tipo '00' flour, for dusting

about 3 tbsp pizza tomato sauce (page 224)

½ tsp fresh thyme leaves

1 buffalo mozzarella ball (250g)

1 salamella sausage, thinly sliced (or any Italian spicy sausage)

50g chorizo slices

2 tbsp freshly grated Parmesan

small handful pecorino shavings

extra virgin olive oil, for drizzling

freshly ground black pepper

SERVES 1

Plenty of stringy cheese and flavoursome spicy sausage – what's not to love? Use chorizo or pepperoni or whatever you can get your hands on. Add more meat if you wish.

Prepare to cook the pizza · Get the dough ready, preheat your oven, shape the dough and prepare the pizza base as described on page 115.

Make the pizza · Spread the pizza tomato sauce to give a thin, even layer on the stretched-out pizza dough, leaving a 2cm border around the edges to create the crust. Scatter over the thyme leaves, then tear or slice the mozzarella and scatter on top. Add the spicy sausage and chorizo. Scatter over the Parmesan and slide into the hot oven, turning the pizza halfway through if you are using an Ooni. In an Ooni on low heat, the pizza should be cooked in 4–6 minutes. In the oven, it should take about 10–12 minutes, depending on how thin or thick the dough is.

Time to serve · Remove the pizza from the oven and slide it on to a dinner plate, then, using a pizza wheel or scissors, cut into slices. Finish with the pecorino, extra virgin olive oil and freshly ground black pepper.

TOMATO, NDUJA AND BURRATA PIZZA WITH HONEY

200g pizza dough ball (see pages 110–112)

Tipo '00' flour, for dusting

about 3 tbsp pizza tomato sauce (page 224)

50g soft onions with thyme, bay leaf and garlic (page 231)

1 ripe tomato, quartered and seeds removed

25g nduja sausage or paste

250g burrata or good ricotta

¼ tsp chopped fresh oregano

2–3 tsp raw honey

small handful pecorino or Parmesan shavings

extra virgin olive oil, for drizzling

SERVES 1

I really enjoy how these new pizza flavours work together. I feel like the burrata just calms everything else down, helped with a little sweetness from the honey.

Prepare to cook the pizza · Get the dough ready, preheat your oven, shape the dough and prepare the pizza base as described on page 115.

Make the pizza · Spread the pizza tomato sauce in a thin, even layer on the stretched-out pizza dough, leaving a 2cm border around the edges to create the crust. Scatter over the soft onions and quartered tomato and spread out small spoonfuls of the nduja. Tear over the burrata or ricotta and sprinkle with oregano, then slide into the hot oven, turning the pizza halfway through if you are using an Ooni. In an Ooni on low heat, the pizza should be cooked in 4–6 minutes. In the oven, it should take about 10–12 minutes, depending on how thin or thick the dough is.

Time to serve · Remove the pizza from the oven and slide it on to a dinner plate, then, using a pizza wheel or scissors, cut into slices. Finish with a drizzle of honey and the pecorino or Parmesan and a drizzle of extra virgin olive oil.

FRIED POTATO, ONION AND ROSEMARY PIZZA

200g pizza dough ball (see
   pages 110–112)
Tipo '00' flour, for dusting
1 baby potato
50ml olive oil
2 garlic cloves
2 fresh thyme sprigs
20g butter
50g béchamel sauce (page 217)
60g soft onions with thyme,
   bay leaf and garlic (page
   231)
3 fresh rosemary sprigs
1 buffalo mozzarella ball
   (250g)
handful Parmesan shavings

SERVES 1

This is one of my favourites, with a white base pizza – a classic marriage of cheese, rosemary and onion. The potato is coloured in the pan first, and it should colour a bit more in the oven.

Prepare to cook the pizza · Get the dough ready, preheat your oven, shape the dough and prepare the pizza base as described on page 115.

Cook the potato · Slice the potato 2mm thick on a mandolin, discarding the ends. Warm a pan with the olive oil, garlic and thyme. Add the potatoes and shallow fry until coloured on one side, then turn over and add the butter. Once the potato slices are evenly coloured, remove from the pan with a slotted spoon.

Make the pizza · Spread the béchamel sauce to give a thin, even layer on the stretched-out pizza dough, leaving a 2cm border around the edges to create the crust. Add small teaspoonfuls of the soft onions, add the fried potato and scatter small rosemary sprigs on top. Tear over the buffalo mozzarella, then slide into the hot oven, turning the pizza halfway through if you are using an Ooni. In an Ooni on low heat, the pizza should be cooked in 4–6 minutes. In the oven, it should take about 10–12 minutes, depending on how thin or thick the dough is.

Time to serve · Remove the pizza from the oven and slide it on to a dinner plate, then, using a pizza wheel or scissors, cut into slices. Finish with the Parmesan shavings.

COMFORT

CURRIES

I think all dads should know how to make a good curry. It's one of those things that, once you get the prep done and cook out the spices, you can pretty much get it all into the pot at once. I've added a few extra bits for when you're feeling a little bit more ambitious, but do stick to the cooking times so the flavours come together perfectly.

COCONUT CHICKEN CURRY WITH CASHEW NUTS

6 garlic cloves, peeled

30g piece fresh root ginger

1 tsp ground cumin

1 tsp ground coriander

1 tbsp Madras curry powder

2 tbsp tomato purée

230ml olive oil

6 chicken legs (thigh and drumstick attached)

50g cashew nuts

1 onion, diced

1 fresh thyme sprig

350ml chicken stock (from a stock cube)

400g tin chopped tomatoes

200ml coconut milk

salt

3 tbsp sugar

good handful fresh coriander leaves

steamed jasmine rice, to serve

SERVES 6

Let the legs cook in the sauce, and add the coconut milk at the end. The classic flavours here are finished with the coriander, lime and cashew nuts.

Make the curry paste · Place the garlic, ginger, cumin, coriander, Madras curry powder, tomato purée and 150ml of the olive oil in a NutriBullet or blender and blend to a smooth paste.

Colour the chicken · Heat 80ml of the oil in a shallow casserole dish or ovenproof sauté pan over a medium heat. Dry the chicken well with kitchen paper, then season with salt. Add to the pan, skin-side down, and sauté until the chicken legs are golden, reducing the heat a little if they begin to colour too quickly. Transfer to a plate.

Roast the cashew nuts · Preheat the oven to 150°C (300°F/Gas Mark 2). Spread the cashew nuts in a small baking tin and roast for 8–10 minutes, until lightly golden, stirring once to ensure they cook evenly. Set aside to cool and increase the oven temperature to 190°C (375°F/Gas Mark 5).

Assemble the curry · Reduce the heat on the pan you used to cook the chicken to low and add the curry paste, then sauté for 1 minute to cook out the spices. Tip in the onion and thyme sprig and cook for about 10 minutes, until the onions are softened and transparent. Stir in the stock and chopped tomatoes and sit the chicken legs on top so that the skin can still crisp up. Bake for 25 minutes, until the chicken is tender and slices off the bone.

Time to serve · Transfer the chicken legs to a platter and keep warm. Stir the coconut milk into the curry sauce and add 1 tablespoon of salt and 3 tablespoons of sugar, then allow to warm through. Add the roasted cashew nuts and pour into a serving dish, then sit the rested chicken legs on top. Scatter over the coriander leaves. Serve with a separate dish of jasmine rice.

BRAISED LAMB RED CURRY WITH MINT YOGHURT

80g Thai red curry paste
5cm piece fresh root ginger, chopped
3 garlic cloves, peeled
210ml vegetable oil
1kg boneless lamb shoulder, well-trimmed and cut into 3cm pieces
1 tbsp salt
2 tsp tomato purée
1 large onion, diced
400g tin chopped tomatoes
1 litre chicken stock (made from 2 chicken jelly stock pots)
500ml water
2 bay leaves
2 tbsp sugar, plus extra pinch
380g Greek yoghurt
5 fresh mint leaves, finely chopped
juice of 1 lime
juice and zest of 1 lemon
3 ripe tomatoes
50g cornflour mixed with 3 tbsp water
2 tbsp toasted flaked almonds
sea salt and freshly ground white pepper
steamed basmati rice, to serve

SERVES 6–8

This curry cooks slowly and becomes more intense as it does. Ask your butcher to give you something with a little bit of fat on it for better flavour, which will make the whole thing taste better as it renders into the sauce. The yoghurt mint dip will soften the intense flavour of the red curry paste.

Make the curry paste · Put the Thai red curry paste in a NutriBullet with the ginger and garlic and 150ml of the vegetable oil and blend to a smooth paste.

Seal the lamb · Put the lamb into a large bowl and season with the salt and mix in 60ml of vegetable oil. Heat a large casserole dish or heavy-based pan over a medium-high heat and, using a tongs, seal the lamb by cooking it in batches until golden brown all over. Transfer back into the bowl.

Make the curry base · In the casserole dish, cook the curry paste with the tomato purée for 1 minute, stirring constantly. Reduce the heat to low, then tip in the onion, stirring to combine. Cover with a lid and cook for 10 minutes to deglaze the bottom of the casserole.

Cook the curry · Add the tinned tomatoes to the onion mixture and increase the heat back up to high, then add back in the lamb with any juices. Add the chicken stock, water and bay leaves, then season with salt and the sugar and bring to the boil. Reduce the heat to low, then cover with a lid and cook for 1 hour.

Make the mint yoghurt · Mix 200g of the yoghurt in a bowl with the mint, lime juice, lemon zest and juice and a pinch of sugar. Season to taste.

Finish the curry · Cut the tomatoes into quarters and remove the seeds, then add to the lamb and cook for another 15 minutes, until the lamb is completely tender but still holding its shape. To finish the curry, whisk the cornflour mixture into the sauce and bring to a simmer to thicken, stirring occasionally. Then stir in the remaining 180g of yoghurt and just warm through. Season to taste.

Time to serve · Scatter the almonds over the braised lamb red curry and bring the casserole straight to the table with a separate bowl of rice and a dish of the mint yoghurt alongside.

ROASTED MONKFISH CURRY WITH LEMONGRASS

25g fresh root ginger (not peeled)

25g garlic cloves, peeled

40g Madras medium curry powder

250ml olive oil

1 large onion, diced

1 fresh thyme sprig

1 bay leaf

40g tomato purée

400g tin coconut milk

1 litre chicken stock (from a stock cube)

1 tsp salt, plus extra for seasoning

1 tsp sugar

160g mooli, peeled and cut into 1cm slices

finely grated rind of 1 lemon

3 lemongrass stalks, halved

3 tomatoes, quartered and seeds removed

4 × 220–240g monkfish portions (see kitchen note)

200g crunchy peanut butter

100g cherry tomatoes, halved and deseeded

150g kale

steamed jasmine rice, to serve

SERVES 4

☕ ☕ ☕

Kitchen Note: *Monkfish holds up beautifully to this type of cooking, and the sauce can be prepped in advance. Ask your fishmonger to remove the skin and keep it on the bone.*

I don't like most fish in curries, but monkfish is meaty and big enough to handle this. The lemongrass adds a layer of freshness, and cooking the fish on the bone makes the whole thing juicier.

Make the curry paste · Put the ginger, garlic and curry powder in a NutriBullet with 150ml of the oil and blend to a smooth paste.

Make the curry sauce · Heat a sauté pan over a medium heat and sauté the curry paste for 2–3 minutes. Add the onion, thyme and bay leaf and sauté for 10 minutes, until the curry paste has cooked out. Reduce the heat, add the tomato purée and cook for 3–4 minutes, stirring. Stir in the coconut milk and stock and season with the salt and sugar. Fold in the mooli, lemon rind and lemongrass, then cover and simmer gently for 30 minutes until the mooli is tender, stirring occasionally to prevent it from sticking. Stir in the tomato quarters and set the sauce aside until needed.

Finish the curry · Preheat the oven to 160°C (320°F/Gas Mark 3). Season the monkfish portions with salt. Heat 100ml of olive oil in a non-stick frying pan over a high heat. Once the pan is sizzling hot, add the monkfish, presentation-side down, and cook for 2–3 minutes until nicely golden. Put the sauce back on the heat and bring to a gentle simmer. Add the monkfish, presentation-side up. The sauce should come halfway up the monkfish – it should not be submerged. Braise in the oven for 10 minutes until tender.

Time to serve · Transfer the monkfish to warm wide-rimmed bowls and leave in a warm place to rest. Whisk the peanut butter into the sauce and check the seasoning, adding a little more salt and sugar if you think it needs it. Fold in the cherry tomatoes and kale and then spoon over the monkfish. Serve with separate bowls of the rice.

TOMATO AND CHICKPEA CURRY

25g garlic cloves, peeled
25g piece fresh root ginger,
    roughly chopped
60g Madras curry powder
25g tomato purée
180ml olive oil
2 large onions, diced
400g tin chickpeas (not
    drained)
300ml apple juice
400g tin chopped tomatoes
3 red apples, peeled, cored and
    chopped
180g golden raisins
1 fresh thyme sprig
1 bay leaf
10 cherry tomatoes, halved
3 ripe tomatoes, cut into
    quarters and deseeded
150g ground almonds
handful fresh coriander leaves
salt and freshly ground black
    pepper
warm flatbreads, to serve
    (optional – see page 211)

SERVES 4

This is delicious as a vegetarian choice, but you could add fish or meat to it as well. I like a bit of fruit in curry, and this has it. The whole thing is even better if you do the flatbreads as well.

Make the curry paste · Place the garlic, ginger, Madras curry powder, tomato purée and 100ml of the olive oil in a NutriBullet and blend to a smooth paste.

Assemble the curry · Heat 80ml of the oil in a heavy-based pan over a medium to high heat. Add the onions and sauté for 8–10 minutes, until softened and transparent. Stir in the curry paste and cook for 1 minute to cook out the spices. Pour in the whole tin of chickpeas with the apple juice and chopped tomatoes. Add the apples, raisins, thyme and bay leaf and bring to a simmer, then reduce the heat and simmer for 40 minutes until the liquid has reduced and the apples have thickened the sauce.

Finish the curry · Add the halved cherry tomatoes and tomato quarters to the curry, then fold in the ground almonds. Season to taste with salt and pepper.

Time to serve · Transfer the chickpea curry to a warmed serving dish and scatter over the coriander leaves. Serve with the flatbreads, if using, allowing everyone to help themselves.

BRAISING

AND

STEWS

I've put together some solid stew recipes here. You'll need to give yourself a bit of time for these, but the slow cooking can be done while you're busy with other things. The techniques here will give you great flavour and rustic, unfussy stews. There's something so nourishing about slow-cooked dishes, with the meat falling apart but still moist – perfect on winter evenings.

NAVARIN OF LAMB

1.5kg boned leg of lamb, cut into large chunks (each about 30g)
200ml olive oil
150g butter
150g carrots, cut into chunks
4 garlic cloves, peeled
1 leek, white part only, thinly sliced (100g)
2 celery sticks, trimmed and thinly sliced (100g)
5 fresh thyme sprigs
5 fresh rosemary sprigs
50g tomato purée
300ml dry white wine
5 bay leaves
10 black peppercorns
400g tin chopped tomatoes
600ml water
1 litre chicken stock (made from 2 chicken jelly stock pots)
1 tbsp chopped fresh flat-leaf parsley
10 cherry tomatoes, halved and deseeded
sea salt and freshly ground black pepper
creamy mashed potatoes, to serve (see page 168)

SERVES 6–8

This is an old-school lamb tomato stew – it reminds me of being a young chef and learning how to braise in the kitchen, but it's perfect for the family at home. Done right, the meat will just fall apart. Serve this unfussy stew with mashed potatoes.

Sear the lamb · Heat a deep casserole dish over a high heat. Season the lamb with salt and pepper. Add half the oil and, once hot, sauté half of the lamb until browned, using a tongs to turn the pieces so that you colour all sides. Transfer the lamb to a plate and, using the remaining oil, repeat for the other half of the lamb.

Cook the casserole · Preheat the oven to 160°C (320°F/Gas Mark 3). Add the butter to the dish and, once foaming, tip in the carrots and garlic, stirring to combine. Add the leek, celery, thyme and rosemary and sauté for 6–8 minutes, until you have a good colouration. Return the sautéed lamb to the pan, with any juices, add the tomato purée and cook for 1 minute, stirring. Pour in the wine and scrape the bottom of the dish to remove any sediment. Allow the liquid to reduce by half and then add the bay leaves, peppercorns, chopped tomatoes, water and stock. Bring to a simmer, then cover with a lid and transfer to the oven for 1 hour 45 minutes, until the lamb is tender but not falling apart.

Reduce the casserole · Strain the sauce from the lamb into a clean pan, discarding all the vegetables except the carrots and the herbs. Bring the juices to the boil over a high heat, then reduce by half and return to the lamb in the original casserole with the reserved carrots. Return to a gentle simmer to warm through, then stir in the parsley and cherry tomatoes. Season to taste.

Time to serve · Serve in shallow wide-rimmed bowls with some of the creamy mashed potatoes.

CRISPY PORK BELLY WITH PEAR AND FENNEL

FOR THE BRINE

1 litre water
200g sea salt
150g demerara sugar
1 tsp black peppercorns
2 whole cloves
2 tsp fennel seeds
2 tsp coriander seeds
2 fresh thyme sprigs
1 bay leaf

FOR THE PORK

1kg piece pork belly
20g fennel seeds
20g coriander seeds
2 carrots, cut into chunks
1 onion, cut into chunks
1 fennel bulb, cut into chunks
4 garlic cloves, peeled
3 fresh thyme sprigs

FOR THE GARNISH

100ml olive oil
2 hard pears, quartered
1 fennel bulb, trimmed and
    quartered
2 tsp sugar
100ml vanilla stock syrup
juice of ½ lemon
20g butter, diced
honey mustard vinaigrette, to
    serve (see page 246)
pear and shallot chutney, to
    serve (see page 240)

SERVES 6–8

The key here is the brine and getting it on the pork in advance. The brine will give you the best crispy pork skin because the salt pulls the moisture from the meat. The pear and the fennel make a lovely accompaniment.

Make the brine · Put the water in a large pan with the sea salt, sugar, spices and herbs. Bring to the boil, stirring to dissolve the sugar and salt, then remove from the heat and leave to cool down to room temperature. Pour into a large rigid container with a lid and add the pork belly – it needs to be fully immersed. Secure the lid and put in the fridge for 12 hours.

Roast the pork belly · Preheat the oven to 150°C (300°F/Gas Mark 2). Heat a heavy-based frying pan over a low heat and toast the fennel and coriander seeds for a couple of minutes until fragrant. Transfer to a coffee grinder and blitz to a fine powder. Remove the pork belly from the brine and lightly dust the meat part with the spice powder. Dry the skin well with kitchen paper and then score using a sharp knife. Put the vegetables in a foil-lined roasting tin, as a trivet, and tuck in the garlic and thyme, then nestle the dusted pork belly on top. Roast for 3 hours, until completely tender with crispy golden-brown skin. Set aside in a warm place to rest for 30 minutes.

Make the garnish · Once the pork is resting, increase the oven temperature to 160°C (320°F/Gas Mark 3). Then heat the oil in an ovenproof frying pan over a medium heat. Add the pear and fennel quarters to the pan and sauté for 5–8 minutes, until coloured on all sides. Sprinkle over the sugar and allow to caramelise. Add the vanilla stock syrup, lemon juice and butter, swirling to combine. Cover with a round of parchment paper and roast for 5 minutes, until the syrup has reduced and the pear and fennel quarters have a nice glaze and are golden brown.

Time to serve · Carve the rested pork belly into slices and arrange on warm plates with the glazed pear and fennel quarters. Drizzle a couple of spoonfuls of honey mustard vinaigrette over the dish, and add a few spoonfuls of the pear and shallot chutney on the side.

IRISH STEW WITH PEARL BARLEY AND LOVAGE

2 tbsp olive oil
1.5kg piece lamb shoulder
6 carrots
4 celery sticks
4 leeks
2 onions, halved
1.7 litres chicken stock (made from 4 chicken jelly stock pots)
400g baby new potatoes
60g pearl barley
6 spring onions, trimmed
8 fresh thyme sprigs
2 bay leaves
good handful fresh flat-leaf parsley leaves, finely chopped
10g fresh lovage, thinly sliced, plus extra to garnish
salt and freshly ground black pepper

SERVES 4–6

I love Irish stew, but I've always had a problem with its timing, which I've changed here. I've also roasted the shoulder for far more flavour. This technique ensures the vegetables and pearl barley aren't overcooked by the time the meat is done. My addition of lovage gives it that recognisable warm hint of celery flavour. It's delicious with some crusty bread or maybe some homemade brown sauce (page 229).

Make the stew base · Preheat the oven to 170°C (325°F/Gas Mark 3). Heat a large casserole pot over a medium to high heat. Add the oil and then sauté the lamb for about 10–15 minutes until coloured. Once you have finished, add two each of the carrots, celery and leeks with the onions. Pour over 1.2 litres of stock, reserving 500ml, and season with salt and pepper. Bring to a simmer, then cover with the lid and cook in the oven for 2 hours, until the lamb is meltingly tender.

Prep the vegetables · Meanwhile, peel the remaining carrots and cut into 4cm slices on the diagonal. Trim the rest of the celery and cut into similar-sized slices. Trim off the green part of the remaining leeks and cut into 4cm chunks.

Prep the lamb · When the lamb is cooked, leave it to rest in the liquid for at least 30 minutes or up to a couple of hours. Remove the lamb shoulder from the pot and put it on a chopping board, then gently pull away the meat from the bone, breaking it into large pieces.

Finish the stew · Add the reserved chicken stock. Add the potatoes and pearl barley to the pot and cook over a high heat for 10 minutes, then reduce the heat to a gentle simmer and add the prepared vegetables, whole spring onions, thyme and bay leaves. Cover with the lid and continue to cook for 45 minutes, then add back in the lamb pieces, parsley and lovage, and simmer for another 5 minutes until the lamb fat melts into the stew to maximise the flavour.

Time to serve · Ladle the Irish stew into bowls and garnish with extra lovage leaves.

FEATHER BLADE BEEF BOURGUIGNON

1kg piece beef feather blade
50g banana shallots, chopped
3 garlic cloves, peeled
3 fresh thyme sprigs
2 bay leaves
1 tbsp white peppercorns
150g carrots, cut into large
   chunks
4 celery sticks, cut into chunks
250ml red wine
6 tbsp/90ml vegetable oil
2 tbsp butter
500ml beef stock (made with
   2 beef jelly stock pots)

FOR THE GARNISH
50g pearl onions, peeled (or 1
   small brown onion, halved)
1 chicken jelly stock pot made
   up with 150ml boiling water
2 garlic cloves, peeled
2 fresh thyme sprigs
4 tbsp vegetable oil
100g smoked bacon lardons
8 white mushrooms, trimmed
1 tbsp chopped fresh flat-leaf
   parsley
sea salt and freshly ground
   black pepper
creamy mashed potatoes, to
   serve (see page 168)

SERVES 6–8

A classic: old-school red-wine-braised beef with smoky bacon and mushrooms, cooked low and slow to let the flavours mature. Any dad that learns how to make this will cook it again and again.

Make the marinade · Cut the feather blade into large chunks, each about 30g, and place in a large non-metallic bowl. Add the shallot, garlic, thyme, bay leaves, peppercorns, carrots and celery, and then pour over the wine. Cover with cling film and chill overnight.

Prepare the beef to cook · Strain the marinated meat into another bowl, using a colander, then pick out the meat pieces and put on a plate lined with kitchen paper, using some more to dry off any excess liquid. Reserve the rest of the vegetables and herbs in the colander, and the marinade in the bowl.

Sear the beef · Heat a shallow casserole dish over a high heat and add two tablespoons of the oil and sauté half of the beef until browned, using a tongs to turn them so that you colour all sides. Transfer the beef to a plate and use another two tablespoons of oil for the rest of the beef.

Cook the casserole · Preheat the oven to 180°C (350°F/Gas Mark 4). Add another 2 tablespoons of oil and 2 tablespoons of butter to the dish and tip in the reserved vegetables and herbs from the marinade. Sauté for 6–8 minutes, until you have a good colouration. Return the sautéed beef with any juices and the wine from the marinade to the dish, then scrape the bottom of the dish to remove any sediment. Allow the liquid to reduce by half and then add the beef stock. Season to taste. Bring to a simmer, then cover with a lid and transfer to the oven for 2 hours, until the meat is really tender but not falling apart. It should be soft to the touch and crushed easily with the back of a spoon.

Cook the garnish · Place the pearl onions in a pan with the chicken stock, garlic, thyme and 1 teaspoon of salt. Bring to a simmer, then cover and cook gently for 5 minutes, then drain. Heat a large non-stick frying pan over a medium heat. Add 4 tablespoons of oil and sauté the bacon and mushrooms for about 5 minutes, until the bacon is starting to crisp and the mushrooms have lightly caramelised. Add the pearl onions and sauté for another 5 minutes, until tender and the garnish is golden brown.

Finish the casserole · Strain the beef from the sauce into a clean pan, discarding the vegetables and herbs. Bring the juices to the boil over a high heat, then reduce by half and return to the beef in the original casserole. Return to a gentle simmer to warm through and stir in the parsley. Season to taste. Scatter the garnish over the beef Bourguignon and serve with a separate bowl of the creamy mashed potatoes.

THE BIG ROAST

I recommend a Sunday, or a day when you have more time, for these recipes. A big roast dinner is ideal for bringing your loved ones together, but spending the morning preparing and then serving it while everything's still hot can be a challenge, so I've tried to limit the amount of pots and pans you'll need to use. You don't have to have lots of things on the plate to make it great and delicious – just simple things done well. I've also included a vegetarian roast here, to give you a little bit more in your arsenal.

ROAST BEEF, YORKSHIRE PUDDING AND GLAZED CARROTS

FOR THE YORKSHIRE PUDDINGS

265ml milk
4 eggs
225g plain flour
1 tsp sea salt flakes
vegetable oil, for cooking
3 tbsp caramelised onion marmalade (page 234)

FOR THE BEEF

1 tbsp mixed peppercorns
1 tbsp sea salt flakes
8 fresh thyme sprigs, leaves stripped
4 fresh rosemary sprigs, leaves stripped
1.5kg beef sirloin
2 tbsp olive oil
vegetable oil, for cooking

FOR THE CARROTS

3 carrots, peeled and thinly sliced into long diagonal strips (on a mandolin)
100ml water
10g softened butter
30g sugar
2 bay leaves
2 fresh tarragon sprigs, 1 whole and one with leaves stripped and finely chopped

FOR THE GRAVY

300ml roast chicken-wing gravy (page 216) or chicken stock
2 tbsp caramelised onion marmalade (page 234)

SERVES 6–8

I'd recommend that you make your Yorkshire pudding mix the day before, as it is better for rising and the yorkies will be more stable.

Make the Yorkshire pudding batter · Whisk the milk and eggs in a large bowl. Sieve in the flour and whisk again until smooth. Cover with cling film and leave to rest in the fridge overnight for best results.

Prepare the beef · Preheat the oven to 170°C (325°F/Gas Mark 3). Put the mixed peppercorns in a coffee grinder with one tablespoon of the salt, the thyme and rosemary. Blitz until everything is finely chopped, then rub it all over the beef and leave it aside for 30 minutes. Then put the beef in a roasting tin and drizzle with the olive oil. Roast for 40 minutes until medium rare. If you have a thermometer, you can check this – the inside temperature should be 55°C. Remove from the oven and cover loosely with tinfoil.

Cook the Yorkshire puddings · Once the beef is cooked and resting, increase the oven temperature to 190°C (375°F/Gas Mark 5). Take a 12-hole muffin tin and pour 1cm of vegetable oil into each hole. Put the tin in the oven for 10 minutes. Remove the batter from the fridge and whisk in the teaspoon of salt with 3 tablespoons of the onion marmalade, then check the consistency – it should just coat the back of a spoon. Remove the tin from the oven and quickly fill each muffin hole two-thirds of the way with the cold batter. Increase the heat to 200°C (400°F/Gas Mark 6) and cook the puddings for 20 minutes, then reduce the temperature to 180°C (350°F/Gas Mark 4) and cook for another 10 minutes, until well risen and golden brown.

Make the glazed carrots · Put the carrots into a pan with the water, butter, sugar, bay leaves and the tarragon sprig. Bring to the boil, then reduce the heat and cover with a circle of parchment paper or a lid. Simmer for 6–8 minutes, until the carrots are tender, nicely glazed and the liquid has reduced. Remove the bay leaves and tarragon sprig and keep the carrots warm, stirring in the chopped tarragon just before serving.

Make the gravy · Transfer the rested beef to a platter for carving and pour off any excess fat from the tin, then put the tin directly on the hob over a medium heat. Pour in the chicken gravy and 2 tablespoons of the caramelised onion marmalade and use it to deglaze the tin, scraping with a wooden spoon to remove all the sediment. Bring to a simmer, stirring continuously, until thickened to your liking. Keep warm.

Time to serve · Carve the beef into slices and arrange on a platter. Have separate dishes of the yorkies and glazed carrots, and serve the gravy in a jug.

LEG OF LAMB WITH HONEY ROAST GARLIC, BABA GHANOUSH AND TOMATO SALAD

2.5kg leg of lamb
10 cloves of honey roast garlic (page 235)
10 fresh rosemary sprigs
about 2 tbsp honey
1 litre chicken stock (made with two chicken jelly stock pots)
2 red onions
4 bay leaves
about 2 tbsp extra virgin olive oil

FOR THE BABA GHANOUSH
1 large aubergine (500g)
100ml olive oil
2 red onions, halved
1 garlic bulb, cut in half
3 tbsp ras el hanout
180ml extra virgin olive oil
50g pitted black olives
2 tbsp honey
4 fresh basil leaves, shredded

FOR THE SALAD
2 ripe beef tomatoes
1 tbsp rinsed baby capers
½ red onion
2–3 tbsp honey mustard vinaigrette (page 246)

sea salt flakes and freshly ground black pepper
duck fat roast potatoes (page 173), to serve

SERVES 6

This is the 'Epic Roast', with a twist on summer flavours. The resting of the lamb is essential for soft and flaky meat.

Roast the lamb · Preheat the oven to 150°C (300°F/Gas Mark 2). Using a sharp knife, score the top of the lamb to create ten holes. The incisions should be about 2cm deep. Squeeze a clove of honey roast garlic and a sprig of rosemary into each hole. Rub the top of the lamb with honey. Add the stock to a roasting tin. Quarter the onions and place in the bottom of the tray, with the bay leaves. Then place the lamb into the stock, top side down. Drizzle with extra virgin olive oil. Cover with tinfoil but don't tighten it too much, as we want some steam to escape. Roast for 4 hours. Remove from the oven, uncover and flip the leg over. Be careful, as it is incredibly tender and likely to want to fall apart at this stage. Return it to the oven for 35–45 minutes, until browned on the underside. Remove from the oven and transfer to a chopping board, then leave to rest for 50 minutes to 1 hour.

Make the baba ghanoush · Cut the aubergine in half lengthways and, using a small sharp knife, score the top of each half in a criss-cross pattern 5cm deep. Heat the olive oil a large frying pan over a medium to high heat and add the aubergine, cut-side down. Cook for 8–10 minutes, until golden brown, then transfer to a foil-lined roasting tin. Add the red onion and garlic and drizzle over 100ml of the extra virgin olive oil. Sprinkle with 2 tablespoons of the ras el hanout and season with salt. Cover tightly with foil and put in the oven at 150°C (300°F/Gas Mark 2) on the top shelf for 45–50 minutes.

Make the tomato salad · Slice the tomatoes very thinly with a sharp knife. Arrange on a plate and sprinkle the capers on top. Using a mandolin, thinly slice the red onion and arrange on top. Dress with the honey mustard vinaigrette and season with salt.

Finish the baba ghanoush · Open the parcel up, transfer the red onions to a plate along with the olives, ready to serve. Roughly chop the aubergine on a chopping board with a large knife and put into a pan. Squeeze in the garlic from the tin and add the remaining ras el hanout and honey. Add the basil and remaining extra virgin olive oil. Season to taste and gently warm through.

Make the gravy · Pass the stock from the roasting tin that you've cooked the lamb in through a sieve into a small pan. Bring to a boil, then a simmer until it's reduced to a gravy consistency. Strip the leaves from a rosemary sprig and finely chop. Stir into the gravy with the honey roast garlic from the lamb..

Time to serve · Carve the lamb into slices and arrange on plates with the roasted red onions. Spoon the baba ghanoush alongside. Pour the gravy into a jug and put on the table with the duck fat roasties and tomato salad.

ROASTED CAULIFLOWER WITH TARRAGON MAYONNAISE

1 cauliflower, leaves removed
  and stalk trimmed (900g)
100ml olive oil
100g butter
3 garlic cloves, peeled
3 fresh thyme sprigs

**FOR THE TARRAGON
MAYONNAISE**
250ml vegetable oil
3 garlic cloves, thinly sliced
60g bunch fresh tarragon, plus
  extra to garnish
150g baby spinach leaves
3 egg yolks
heaped ½ tsp Dijon mustard
2 tsp white wine vinegar
juice and finely grated zest of
  ½ lemon
salt and freshly ground white
  pepper

SERVES 3-4

This is a great vegetarian choice, and still very much a roast. The nutty flavour of the brown butter works really well with the cauliflower. You could use this as a sharing plate for the table as well.

Roast the cauliflower · Preheat the oven to 220°C (425°F/Gas Mark 7). Heat an ovenproof pan over a high heat. Season the cauliflower all over. Add the oil to the pan and, once hot, colour the cauliflower on all sides for 5–10 minutes. Add the butter and garlic and thyme, and baste continuously like a roast for five minutes while the butter is melting and sizzling. Put in the oven and roast for 10 minutes. Then turn it over and roast for another 6 minutes, until the cauliflower is completely tender. Check with a long thin metal skewer – it should go in with no resistance.

Make the tarragon oil · Put 200ml of the oil in a small pan and heat to 70–80°C (158–176°F). In a separate pan, add the remaining 50ml of the oil and cook the garlic over a low heat for a minute or two, until tender but with no colour. Add the tarragon and cook for 20 seconds, then add the spinach and cook for another 30 seconds. Remove from the heat and stir in the rest of the warm oil. Pour into a blender and blend until smooth, then pass through a fine sieve and set aside. You should be left with a green oil.

Make the tarragon mayonnaise · Mix the egg yolks with the mustard, vinegar, 2–3 spoonfuls of warm water, the lemon zest and a good pinch of salt. Pour the tarragon oil into a jug. Use an electric whisk, or balloon whisk with plenty of elbow grease, to whisk the egg-yolk mixture, then very slowly drip in the tarragon oil. When the mixture is thicker and no oil is visible, swap the drip to a slow, steady stream – whisking all the time.

Flavour the mayonnaise · When all the oil is added and you have a smooth, thick mayonnaise, taste and season with salt and pepper. Stir in the lemon juice.

Time to serve · Transfer the roasted whole cauliflower to a serving plate, put a bowl of the tarragon mayonnaise alongside, and garnish with extra tarragon.

CHICKEN BASQUAISE WITH SPICY SAUSAGE

1 large chicken
140g plain flour
2½ tsp garlic powder
4 tsp smoked paprika
4 tsp sweet paprika
2 tsp espelette pepper
160ml sunflower or vegetable
  oil
1 salamella sausage, peeled
  and cut into 1cm slices
  (Italian spicy sausage)
2 garlic cloves, chopped
1 large onion, chopped
3 fresh thyme sprigs
3 bay leaves
2 × 400g tins chopped
  tomatoes
2 red peppers, cut into
  quarters with core and
  seeds removed
2 tbsp chopped fresh flat-leaf
  parsley
sea salt flakes and freshly
  ground white pepper

SERVES 4–6

This chicken dish from the Basque region is a fantastic alternative to a Sunday roast. Once you cut up the chicken, it cooks quite quickly, and as the juices seep into the red pepper stew, the skin becomes crispy on top. Perfect with some simple cooked white rice.

Prep the chicken · Put the chicken breast-side down on a chopping board and, using a large sharp knife, cut either side of the parson's nose, releasing the oysters. Then turn back over and cut between the drumstick and breast, holding the thigh to the carcass. On both sides, pull off the thighs to release them from the carcass, then divide each one into two pieces. Cut through the breastbone, cutting through the ribs, then tuck the wing tips behind them and cut each breast into two pieces.

Season the chicken · Mix the flour in a shallow dish with the garlic powder, one tablespoon each of the smoked and sweet paprika and half the espelette pepper. Toss in the chicken pieces, shaking off any excess. Heat 60ml of the sunflower or vegetable oil in a sauté pan over a medium-high heat, and quickly colour the chicken pieces, turning them regularly with a tongs. Remove to a plate and keep warm.

Cook the chicken · Preheat the oven to 170°C (325°F/Gas Mark 3). Heat the rest of the oil in a shallow casserole dish and sauté the salamella sausage and garlic until sizzling. Add the onion with the thyme and bay leaves and sauté for another 10 minutes. Stir in the rest of the smoked and sweet paprika and cook for another 20 seconds, stirring continuously. Mix in the tomatoes and add the red peppers, then season with salt and pepper. Sit the chicken pieces back into the dish – the skin should not be covered so that it can crisp up nicely. Bake for 22 minutes, until the chicken is tender.

Finish the dish · Remove the chicken from the oven and transfer to a plate, then scatter over the rest of the espelette pepper. Fold the parsley into the tomato ragu and then put the chicken back on the ragu and return to the oven for another 2 minutes to make sure the skin is crispy. Serve straight to the table.

PORK, APRICOT AND ROSEMARY STUFFING IN PUFF PASTRY

225g sausage meat

100ml olive oil

100g butter, chilled and diced, plus 2-3 tbsp

6 garlic cloves, thinly sliced (on a mandolin)

2 large onions, finely diced (350g)

5 fresh thyme sprigs, leaves stripped off

200g dried apricots, sliced

80ml brandy or vanilla stock syrup (page 254)

400g brioche

1 tbsp fresh rosemary leaves, finely chopped, plus extra sprigs to garnish

1½ tsp chopped fresh sage

60g bunch fresh flat-leaf parsley, leaves stripped off and finely chopped

2 × 375g sheets ready-rolled puff pastry, thawed if frozen

plain flour, for dusting

4 eggs mixed with 4 tsp water (egg wash)

sea salt flakes and freshly ground white pepper

duck fat roasties (page 173) and roast chicken-wing gravy (page 216), to serve

SERVES 6-8

This can be served as a main roast or to accompany something else. I'm a big fan of stuffing – I love the sweetness of the apricots with the rosemary here. The pork is chopped, so it doesn't become too dense, and the brioche crumbs add a bit of luxury but it's still simple for the kids. Perfect with our chicken gravy.

Start the filling · Break up the sausage meat into pieces. Heat a large non-stick frying pan over a medium to high heat. Add the oil, then reduce the heat to low and sauté the sausage pieces until golden brown all over. Add 100g of butter and once it is foaming add the garlic, tossing to combine. Add the onion and thyme and then cover with a lid. Continue to sauté for 10–15 minutes, until the onions have softened and are transparent, shaking the pan occasionally. Remove from the heat.

Flavour the filling · Put the apricots in a small pan with the brandy or vanilla stock syrup and simmer over a low heat until the liquid has been reduced by half. Stir into the sausage-and-onion mixture and season with salt and pepper. Leave to cool down completely.

Finish the filling · Put the brioche into a food processor and pulse until you have achieved breadcrumbs – they should be quite chunky and not too fine for the best results. Tip into a large bowl and set aside. Add the cooled-down sausage mixture to the food processor, and pulse until roughly chopped, then add it to the brioche crumbs with the rosemary, sage and parsley. Mix well to combine with your hands and with the help of a spatula.

Shape the filling · Lay a layer of cling film on a clean work surface and tip out half the sausage mixture, then shape into a log that is about 30cm long and 10cm wide, making sure not to press it down too much so that the stuffing stays nice and crumbly and you keep the texture of the brioche crumbs. Then scatter over about 2–3 tablespoons of butter in small pieces, and then lay the rest of the sausage mixture on top of the butter, shaping it into a larger log. Wrap the cling film around it tightly and secure the ends, then put on a tray and chill for at least 1 hour or up to 24 hours.

Shape the roll · Take a large baking sheet and dust lightly with flour, then unroll one of the puff pastry sheets. Brush with some of the egg wash, then unroll the chilled stuffing and place it on top. Brush with a little more of the egg wash and then cover with another unrolled piece of puff pastry. Trim down to a nice, neat shape and secure the edges by pinching them with your fingers. Prick the top a few times with a toothpick then brush with more egg wash. Use the excess puff pastry to make decorations, then stick them on and brush with more egg wash. Cover with cling film once the egg wash has dried and set and place in the fridge to chill and rest for 30 minutes or up to 24 hours.

Time to cook · Preheat the oven to 210°C (410°F/Gas Mark 7). Put the stuffing roll in the oven for 20 minutes. Reduce the temperature to 160°C (320°F/Gas Mark 3) and bake for another 15 minutes, until the pastry is cooked through and golden brown.

Time to serve · Leave the stuffing roll to settle for 10 minutes, garnish with rosemary sprigs, then cut into slices and arrange on warm plates with the duck fat roast potatoes and gravy.

BARBECUE

Dads are often relied on for the barbecue – something I know a lot of men enjoy, weather permitting. A good barbecue rub, a tasty glaze for basting the meat and plenty of sauces that can be served cold so you don't have to warm up lots of pans are the order of the day here. With these recipes, you'll be able to lift your barbecue flavour skills to a new height.

HOT HONEY CAJUN CHICKEN DRUMSTICKS

290ml Frank's Hot Sauce
50g tomato ketchup
4 tbsp honey
50g dark brown sugar
1kg chicken drumsticks
80g Cajun spice
1 tbsp sea salt flakes

SERVES 6–8

These are spicy, sweet and sticky – all the essential barbecue flavours.

Make the sauce · Put the hot sauce in a small pan with the ketchup, honey and sugar. Bring to a simmer, stirring until the sugar has dissolved. Remove from the heat.

Season the chicken · Put the chicken drumsticks in a large bowl and sprinkle over the Cajun spice and salt, tossing to coat.

Prepare the barbecue · If using a charcoal barbecue, you'll need one with a lid and to light it at least 1½ hours before you want to start cooking. For it to be ready, the coals need to be completely covered in a layer of white ash. If using a gas barbecue, light it 10 minutes beforehand – the heat needs to be between 150°C (300°F) and 200°C (400°F).

Cook the chicken · Add the chicken drumsticks to the barbecue grill, and give them a good char, turning regularly. Then transfer the charred drumsticks into a large foil container and pour over 120ml of the sauce, rolling to coat. Put the container on the barbecue, cover with the lid and cook for 25 minutes or until the chicken is tender, basting occasionally.

Time to serve · Heat the rest of the sauce for 1–2 minutes in a small pan over a medium heat. Transfer the drumsticks to a warm platter and drizzle over some of the reduced sauce from the container, then pour the rest of the sauce into a dipping bowl and serve alongside.

STICKY SPICED PORK RIBS

2 × 500g meaty pork rib racks
50g English mustard
30g barbecue spice rub (page 228)
300ml barbecue glaze (page 225)
200ml water, plus extra as necessary

SERVES 4–6

Get plenty of mustard on the ribs first here. Give them a good charring, and if the barbecue is too hot, transfer the glazed ribs to an oven – they will cook just fine.

Prepare the meat · Pull off and discard the thick membrane that runs along the back of the ribs, like a fat. Then, using your hands, rub over the English mustard. Sprinkle with a good dusting of the barbecue spice rub, pressing it into the mustard to help it stick. Cover with cling film and leave at room temperature to marinate for 1 hour.

Prepare the barbecue · If using a charcoal barbecue, you'll need one with a lid and to light it at least 1½ hours before you want to start cooking. For it to be ready the coals need to be completely covered in a layer of white ash. If using a gas barbecue, light it 10 minutes beforehand – the heat needs to be between 180°C (350°F) and 200°C (400°F).

Seal the meat · Add the ribs to the barbecue and cook until you've given them a good char, turning regularly.

Finish cooking the meat · If your barbecue doesn't have a lid, preheat the oven to 170°C (325°F/Gas Mark 3). Heat the glaze in a small pan. Transfer each rack of ribs to a large sheet of parchment paper and brush with some of the glaze, pouring the remainder on top. Close up the parchment and make each one into a parcel, ensuring they're tightly sealed so no water can get in. Put the parcels into a large roasting tin and pour around the water. Cover in a foil tent and bake in the preheated oven for 2½ hours or use the barbecue and close the lid, adding extra water as needed – it's important that it never dries out.

Time to serve · Carefully open the parcels – the ribs should be meltingly tender with the meat almost falling off the bone. Transfer the ribs to a warm platter. Drain off the glaze and spoon away any excess fat, then place the remainder in a small pan over a low heat till it's reduced to a sticky glaze. Pour the glaze over the ribs to serve.

SLOW BARBECUE PULLED PORK

2kg piece pork belly

1 tsp sea salt flakes

25g barbecue spice rub (page 228)

550ml barbecue glaze (page 225)

300ml fresh pineapple juice (or from a carton is fine)

8–12 burger buns, split in half (page 207)

pickled cucumber, to serve (page 94)

SERVES 8–12

Cook this slow and low in the glaze, then crush all that top fat with a fork at the end. Perfect in burger buns or served with some of the pickled cucumbers.

Marinate the meat · Using a sharp knife, make an incision under the skin, with your knife parallel to the board, pulling off the top layer of skin of the pork belly. You don't have to be too precise – just get the skin off, as it's tough and will need to be cooked under the pork belly. Rub the rest of the pork belly with salt and then rub the barbecue spice rub all over. Leave at room temperature to marinate for 10 minutes. Put the skin that has been trimmed off in the base of a foil tray.

Prepare the barbecue · If using a charcoal barbecue, you'll need one with a lid and to light it at least 1½ hours before you want to start cooking. For it to be ready, the coals need to be completely covered in a layer of white ash. If using a gas barbecue, light it 10 minutes beforehand – the heat needs to be at least at 180°C (350°F).

Sear the meat · Seal the pork belly on both sides on the barbecue over the hot coals, giving it a good char and loads of colour, turning regularly with a tongs. Meanwhile, heat the barbecue glaze in a small pan. Transfer the sealed pork belly to the foil tray, fat-side down on top of the skin. Pour over the glaze, making sure the joint is well covered, and then pour around the pineapple juice and 250ml water. Cover with tinfoil.

Slow cook the meat · Place the foil-covered tray on the barbecue, close the lid and cook over medium coals (160°C/320°F) for 2 hours and 45 minutes, until the pork belly is meltingly tender and can be easily shredded with a fork. If your barbecue doesn't have a lid, you can also cook it in a preheated oven at 170°C (325°F/Gas Mark 3). Check every 40 minutes to ensure the liquid has not reduced too much – if it has, just top it up with a little more water to prevent it from drying out.

Time to serve · When the pork is cooked, remove the tinfoil. When it has cooled slightly, crush the fat with a fork, breaking it up, then fold it back into the lean meat. Make sure that all of the fat and the liquid is mixed together for the best flavour. Drain the remaining glaze from the foil tray into a small pan, then put over a low heat until reduced to a nice sticky glaze. Fold the reduced barbecue glaze into the shredded pork. Toast the burger buns on the barbecue, then fill with the pulled pork and some cucumber pickle to serve.

CHARRED PICANHA OF BEEF WITH CHIMICHURRI

1kg picanha roast (ask your butcher, or sirloin will do)
sea salt flakes and freshly ground black pepper
200g fresh herb green chimichurri (page 221)
triple-cooked chips, to serve (page 174)

SERVES 6

A perfect way to use up some of your jarred chimichurri. The meat is marinated for 30 minutes to an hour, then the fat is rendered low on the barbecue. After it's cooked, it's rested before slicing for the best results. Other cuts like sirloin and rib eye will work the same.

Marinate the meat · Cut the picanha in half lengthways, season with salt and pepper, then brush the meat all over with about 4 tablespoons of the chimichurri. Leave at room temperature to marinate for 1 hour.

Prepare the barbecue · If using a charcoal barbecue, you'll need one with a lid and to light it at least 1½ hours before you want to start cooking. For it to be ready, the coals need to be completely covered in a layer of white ash. If using a gas barbecue, light it 10 minutes beforehand – the heat needs to be between 160°C and 200°C.

Cook the meat · Place the picanha, fat-side down, on the barbecue over the medium-hot coals and close the lid. Char it for 10–15 minutes, turning every five minutes, then remove and place on a layer of tinfoil to catch the fat. Then cook with the lid down for another 10–15 minutes. Rest the meat off the heat for 15 minutes before carving.

Time to serve · Transfer the picanha to a platter and brush all over with some more of the chimichurri. Then carve into thin slices, arrange on plates and drizzle over a generous amount of the chimichurri. The remainder can be served in a bowl alongside a dish of the triple-cooked chips.

BEEF SLIDERS WITH SMOKED CHEESE, SALSA VERDE AND CHIMICHURRI

600g–800g côte de boeuf (or use rib eye steak, no bone)

2 tbsp barbecue spice rub (page 228)

2 × batches burger buns (8 in each, still stuck together)

1 quantity confit garlic (page 237)

8–16 slices smoked Cheddar cheese (Applewood)

1 quantity salsa verde (page 220)

1 quantity green chimichurri (page 221)

triple-cooked chips (page 174), to serve

SERVES 4

Once everything is made, building this is relatively easy, but the flavour is great. Kids will love these – they'll add something exciting to your barbecue.

Prepare the barbecue · If using a charcoal barbecue, you'll need one with a lid and to light it at least 1½ hours before you want to start cooking. For it to be ready, the coals need to be completely covered in a layer of white ash. If using a gas barbecue, light it 10 minutes beforehand – the heat needs to be between 180°C (350°F) and 200°C (400°F).

Cook the beef · Sprinkle the beef all over with the spice rub and allow it to come up to room temperature. Barbecue over medium-hot coals for 8 minutes for medium rare. Remove from the grill and leave to rest on a plate in a warm place for 10 minutes, before carving into thin slices.

Toast the buns · Split the burger buns and put on the barbecue, cut-side down, for a minute or so until lightly toasted.

Build the sliders · Spread the confit garlic on the bottoms of the toasted burger buns, then pile on the beef slices, cover with the cheese, and add a spoonful of either salsa verde or chimichurri on top of each slider. Cover with the burger-bun tops.

Cook the sliders · Place the sliders in a tinfoil tray and put back on the barbecue, then cover with the lid and cook for 3–4 minutes, until the cheese is melted and bubbling.

Time to serve · Arrange the beef sliders on warm plates with some triple-cooked chips and have dishes with the remaining salsa verde and the chimichurri alongside.

SEA BREAM WITH TIGER BITE SAUCE AND LETTUCE TACOS

500g whole sea bream
25g plain flour
100ml extra virgin olive oil,
    plus extra for brushing
1 bunch spring onions, well-
    trimmed
1 butterhead lettuce
225g ice cubes
good pinch Maldon sea salt
1 small lemon, cut into slices
few spoonfuls kimchi (page
    239)
few spoonfuls spring onion and
    ginger relish (page 241)
1 cucumber, cut on a mandolin
    into strips

**FOR THE TIGER BITE
SAUCE**
200g cherry tomatoes
1 tsp olive oil
1 banana shallot, chopped
2 garlic cloves, chopped
2 red chillies, chopped
60g fresh coriander, chopped
juice of 1 lime
2 tsp Thai fish sauce (nam pla)
1 tsp oyster sauce

SERVES 2

There's a bit of prep here but it's a lovely way to eat this fish.

Make the tiger bite sauce · Toss the cherry tomatoes in olive oil in a baking tin and char with a blowtorch or flash under a hot grill until nicely charred. Set aside to cool a little. Put the shallot, garlic and chillies into a pestle and mortar and bash until finely crushed. Add the coriander and continue to bash until it is evenly combined. Transfer to a bowl and stir in the lime juice, Thai fish and oyster sauces. Take the charred cherry tomatoes and squish them into the sauce with your hands, then give everything another good stir. Cover with cling film and set aside at room temperature to allow the flavours to develop.

Prepare the barbecue · If using a charcoal barbecue, you'll need one with a lid and to light it at least 1½ hours before you want to start cooking. For it to be ready, the coals need to be completely covered in a layer of white ash. If using a gas barbecue, light it 10 minutes beforehand – the heat needs to be between 150°C (300°F) and 180°C (350°F).

Prepare the fish · Clean the sea bream, remove the scales by scraping them from tail to head with a large blunt knife and cut off the fins. Rinse under cold running water and dry with kitchen paper. Cut three deep slashes into both sides of the fish, then dust in the flour, shaking off any excess.

Cook the fish · Brush the grill of the barbecue very well with oil to ensure that the fish will not stick, then add the sea bream over medium coals and cook for 4–6 minutes. Turn over and continue to cook for another 6–8 minutes, until the fish is fully cooked and nicely charred, turning occasionally. Add the spring onions for the last couple of minutes and turn them regularly.

Prepare the lettuce · Discard the outer leaves of the lettuce, then separate the inner leaves and put into a large bowl of water with the ice cubes to crisp up. Just before serving, drain and dry quickly on kitchen paper.

Finish the fish · Put the sea bream into a foil container, pour over the oil, then season with salt and cover with the lemon slices. Close the barbecue lid and cook for 5–10 minutes. When it is ready, the bone will come cleanly away from the head with no resistance. Remove the lemon slices, pour away the excess oil, then gently flake the flesh, making sure no bones remain, and squeeze over the lemon juice.

Time to serve · Spoon a little of the kimchi into the lettuce leaves and add a small mound of the sea bream. Top with a little of the spring onion and ginger relish and a spoonful of the tiger bite sauce. Roll up like a taco and serve with charred spring onions and cucumber slices alongside.

SIDE

CARS

Here I've put together a collection of useful, pretty simple sides that you can use again and again with all kinds of mains. It features plenty of spuds and veggies, with a little salad that converts to a main course if required.

CREAMY MASHED POTATOES

600g–800g large baking
   potatoes (such as Rooster)
about 165g butter, diced, plus
   extra to garnish
150ml milk
1 tsp sea salt
freshly ground white pepper,
   to taste
pinch of freshly grated nutmeg
   (optional)

SERVES 4–6

I often get asked how to do creamed mashed potatoes like in a restaurant, so I thought I'd include the recipe we use here. The potatoes are weighed when cooked, and about a third of that weight in butter is folded back into the warm mashed potatoes. The potatoes will split, but are brought back together with warm milk and finished with salt and ground white pepper. Properly seasoned mashed potatoes are a special thing!

Cook the potatoes · Preheat the oven to 180°C (350°F/Gas Mark 4). Pierce the potatoes a few times to prevent them from bursting, then bake directly on the oven shelf for 1 hour, until soft when gently squeezed.

Mash the potatoes · Remove the potatoes from the oven and cut in half, then, using a spoon, scoop out the flesh and put it into a bowl. Mash with a potato ricer or Mouli and weigh the results. For 400g potato flesh, add 165g butter, then mash it in until the mashed potatoes have split.

Flavour the potatoes · Meanwhile, heat the milk in a small pan to just warm through. Using a spatula or wooden spoon, stir it into the mash until the mix is silky and smooth again. Add the salt and season to taste with the pepper, adding a little nutmeg if liked.

Time to serve · Garnish the creamy mashed potatoes with an extra knob of butter, which will melt into the mash, to serve.

CHAMP POTATOES

600g large baking potatoes
(such as Rooster)
150g butter
2 bunches spring onions,
trimmed and very finely
sliced (only the green parts)
150ml cream
150ml milk
sea salt and freshly ground
white pepper

SERVES 4-6

Champ was everywhere in Belfast when I was growing up – it's like the northern version of colcannon, and it's difficult to call which is the best. Make sure to cut the spring onions super thin and cook them in the cream – delicious.

Cook the potatoes · Preheat the oven to 180°C (350°F/Gas Mark 4). Pierce the potatoes a few times to prevent them from bursting and bake directly on the oven shelf for 1 hour, until soft when gently squeezed.

Mash the potatoes · Remove the potatoes from the oven and cut in half, then, using a spoon, scoop out the flesh into a bowl. Mash with a potato ricer or Mouli and weigh the results – you need 400g in total. Cover with a clean tea towel in a bowl to keep warm.

Make the champ base · Melt 50g of the butter in a large heavy-based pan over a low heat. Add the spring onions and cook for 2 minutes until softened with no change in colour. Pour in the cream and simmer for 2 minutes to slightly reduce. Pour in the milk and bring to a bare simmer.

Time to serve · Fold the mashed potatoes into the spring onion mixture, then beat in the rest of the butter and season to taste with salt and pepper.

COLCANNON POTATOES

600g large baking potatoes
(such as Rooster)
20g curly kale, tough stalks
removed
20g black kale, tough stalks
removed
140g butter
50ml olive oil
1 small onion, finely chopped
(100g)
2 shallots, finely chopped
(200g)
1 fresh thyme sprig, leaves
removed
100ml milk
100ml cream
2 spring onions, very finely
sliced
1 tsp sea salt
sea salt and freshly ground
white pepper

SERVES 4-6

My grandfather was a chef in the Irish army – I suppose knowing that had an influence on me. He was one of my first male role models. This classic Irish dish, one that I know he cooked for his big family, still reminds me of him.

Cook the potatoes · Preheat the oven to 180°C (350°F/Gas Mark 4). Pierce the potatoes a few times to prevent them from bursting and bake directly on the oven shelf for 1 hour, until soft when gently squeezed.

Prepare the kale · Bring a large pan of salted water to the boil and fill a large bowl with ice cold water. Add the curly kale to the pan and cook for 2–3 minutes, then immediately plunge into the bowl of iced water. Drain and dry off any excess water with kitchen paper, then finely chop. Repeat the same process with the black kale.

Mash the potatoes · Remove the potatoes from the oven and cut in half, then, using a spoon, scoop out the flesh into a bowl. Mash with a potato ricer or Mouli and weigh the results – you need 400g in total. Beat in 125g of the butter, then cover with a clean tea towel in a bowl to keep warm.

Make the colcannon base · Melt the remaining knob of butter in a large heavy-based pan with the oil over a low heat. Add the onion, shallots and thyme leaves and cook for 4 minutes, until the onion and shallot have softened. Pour in the milk and cream, then fold in the spring onions and the curly and black kale. Season with the salt. Increase the heat and bring to the boil, then reduce the heat and simmer for 2–3 minutes.

Time to serve · Fold the mashed potatoes into the kale mixture and season to taste with salt and pepper.

DUCK FAT ROAST POTATOES

10 even-sized Maris Piper
   potatoes, peeled and halved
400g duck fat
6 garlic cloves (not peeled)
4 fresh thyme sprigs
sea salt flakes or barbecue
   spice rub (page 228)

SERVES 4-6

The key here is to slightly overcook the potatoes. Use Maris Piper if you can, and let them dry in the air after boiling so they become floury. Duck fat is available in most supermarkets now, so it should be easy enough to pick up. It has a unique flavour, and with the garlic and thyme, it scents the potatoes really well and brings that perfect crispiness. These are my go-to for a Sunday roast or Christmas dinner.

Cook the potatoes · Put the potatoes into a large pan of salted water and bring to the boil. Reduce the heat and partly cover, then simmer gently for 50 minutes or until the edges of the potatoes have started to break down. Drain well and spread out on a tray, then leave to air dry for 1 hour. For best results, leave in the fridge overnight.

Roast the potatoes · Preheat the oven to 180°C (350°F/Gas Mark 4). Once the oven is hot, put a large roasting tin with the duck fat in it and leave it to heat for 20–30 minutes. Once the oil is hot, carefully remove the tin from the oven and add the potatoes, turning quickly to coat. Tuck in the garlic and thyme, then season with salt and roast for 1 hour to 1½ hours or until very crisp and golden brown, turning regularly with a slotted spoon.

Time to serve · Take the roast potatoes out of the fat with a slotted spoon, quickly drain any excess oil off with kitchen paper, then pile high in a warm serving dish. Season with salt or barbecue spice rub.

TRIPLE-COOKED CHIPS

1kg potatoes
vegetable oil, for deep-frying
salt, to taste
malt vinegar, to taste

SERVES 4-6

These are the ultimate crispy chips. Try to find Maris Pipers or look for something that says it fries well on the bag. When blanching, allow them to slightly overcook, then dry them in the air. The two temperatures of the oil is the secret to getting them really crispy.

Prepare the chips · Peel the potatoes and cut into thick chips about 5cm long and 1.5cm thick. Rinse them in cold water to remove as much starch as possible, then put into a large pan – make sure the chips have plenty of room so you can take them out easily.

Blanch the chips · Cover the chips with plenty of cold water and slowly bring to the boil. Simmer gently for 20 minutes, until tender when pierced with a sharp knife and the edges have started to break down. Using a slotted spoon, carefully remove the chips and drain on kitchen paper. Spread out on a cooking rack set over a tray and place warm into the fridge for at least an hour, or overnight for best results.

Deep-fry the chips · Heat a deep-fat fryer with oil to 140°C (275°F). Fry the chips in a couple of batches until they have developed a crust but not taken on any colour – this will take about 5 minutes. Remove each batch and drain on kitchen paper.

Time to serve · Now heat the oil to 190°C (375°F). Return the chips to the deep fat fryer, again in a couple of batches, and cook for 1–2 minutes until they are super crispy and deep golden brown. Drain on kitchen paper and sprinkle with salt and vinegar.

TEMPURA BROCCOLI WITH MISO MAYONNAISE

8–10 tenderstem broccoli
handful of ice cubes
vegetable oil, for deep-frying
100g plain flour
300ml tempura batter (page 222)
20g toasted sesame seeds
200g miso mayonnaise (page 249)
sea salt flakes

SERVES 1-2

I love frying the broccoli in this really crispy batter. It introduces the kids to vegetables cooked in a way they probably wouldn't expect but hopefully will appreciate. The miso mayo is the perfect dip, and the sesame seeds add an Asian flair.

Blanch the broccoli · Bring a large pan of water to the boil and cook the broccoli for 4 minutes, until soft but still green. Using a slotted spoon, transfer it to a bowl of iced water to refresh. When cold enough, drain well and dry on kitchen paper.

Make the tempura · Heat the oil in the deep-fat fryer to 180°C (350°F). Put the flour in a shallow dish and toss in the broccoli, shaking off any excess, then quickly dip into the tempura batter and cook for 5–6 minutes or until crisp and golden brown, turning halfway through with a tongs to ensure they colour evenly. Quickly drain on kitchen paper and season with salt.

Time to serve · Pile the tempura broccoli on to a plate and scatter over the toasted sesame seeds. Have a bowl of miso mayonnaise alongside for dipping.

CHARRED TENDERSTEM BROCCOLI WITH CONFIT GARLIC AND TOASTED ALMONDS

8–10 tenderstem broccoli
handful of ice cubes
30g white miso
130ml honey mustard
  vinaigrette (page 246)
100ml extra virgin olive oil
10 cloves of confit garlic (page
  237)
50g toasted flaked almonds
salt

SERVES 1-2

Charring the broccoli in the pan rather than just boiling it adds an extra dimension of flavour. With the honey mustard dressing, toasted almonds and confit garlic as well, this is definitely moreish.

Blanch the broccoli · Bring a large pan of water to the boil with a tablespoon of salt and cook the broccoli for 4 minutes. Using a slotted spoon, transfer it to a bowl of iced water. Drain well and dry on kitchen paper.

Make the dressing · Put the white miso and vinaigrette in a bowl and whisk until smooth.

Cook the broccoli · Heat a large non-stick frying pan over a high heat. Add the olive oil and, once it is hot, tip in the broccoli and season with salt. Cook the broccoli until nicely charred, turning regularly with a tongs. Add in the confit garlic and roast with the broccoli, but be careful as it will colour quickly. You want a nice dark brown colour on the broccoli. Quickly drain on kitchen paper to remove the excess oil.

Time to serve · Place the warm broccoli and garlic in a bowl and add four to five spoonfuls of the dressing, then toss until evenly coated. Arrange on a warm platter and scatter with the flaked almonds, and add another drizzle of dressing to finish.

ROASTED CARROTS IN CHIMICHURRI WITH LEMON YOGHURT

200g carrots (with green tops)
50ml olive oil
50g butter
4 garlic cloves, peeled
2 bay leaves
2 fresh thyme sprigs
50g fresh herb green
  chimichurri (page 221)

**FOR THE ROASTED
PUMPKIN SEEDS**
100ml water
200g sugar
50g pumpkin seeds

FOR THE LEMON YOGHURT
80g lemon mayonnaise (page
  247)
120g Greek strained yoghurt
  (10% fat)
finely grated zest of 1 lemon
1 tbsp caster sugar

salt and freshly ground white
  pepper

SERVES 1–2

Carrots can be quite boring when they're just boiled, so here they're kept whole and roasted with some aromatics. Then they're rolled in chimichurri and served on top of lemon yoghurt, which adds a freshness to the whole dish.

Make the lemon yoghurt · Put the lemon mayonnaise in a bowl with the yoghurt and lemon zest. Add the sugar and a pinch of salt, then stir well to combine. Cover with cling film and chill until needed.

Roast the pumpkin seeds · Preheat the oven to 180°C (350°F/Gas Mark 4). Put the water and sugar in a heavy-based pan and bring up from cold to hot so that the sugar dissolves. Stir in the pumpkin seeds and cook for 30 seconds, then, using a slotted spoon, drain and put in a small non-stick baking tin. Roast for 12–15 minutes, until caramelised. Remove from the oven and set aside to cool and harden.

Roast the carrots · Reduce the oven temperature to 170°C (325°F/Gas Mark 3). Wash the carrots well, but do not peel. Trim down the green tops with a scissors or knife and reserve to use as a garnish. Heat a large ovenproof frying pan over a high heat. Add the oil, and once it is hot, tip in the carrots and cook for a couple of minutes until they have started to colour. Add the butter, garlic, bay leaves and thyme and season with salt and pepper, then continue to cook for a minute or so with the foaming butter. Transfer to the oven and roast for 15 minutes until the carrots are completely tender and lightly charred.

Time to serve · Remove the roasted carrots from the oven and transfer to kitchen paper to drain off the excess oil, then roll in two tablespoons of the fresh herb green chimichurri. Spread the lemon yoghurt on to small plates and add the rolled carrots. Drizzle over the rest of the fresh herb green chimichurri and scatter over the roasted pumpkin seeds and reserved carrot tops.

GRILLED PEACH AND GREEN BEAN SALAD WITH PICKLED SHALLOTS AND ALMONDS

200g green beans
2 tbsp salt
3 firm, ripe peaches
30g light brown sugar
100ml water
3 tbsp honey mustard
   vinaigrette (page 246)
20g rocket
20g toasted flaked almonds

**FOR THE PICKLED
SHALLOTS**
100g sugar
100g cider vinegar or white-
   wine vinegar
300ml water
100ml olive oil
1 garlic clove, peeled
2 fresh thyme sprigs
2 shallots, peeled and cut into
   3cm rings

SERVES 4

This can be served as a side salad, or you could add some torn burrata to make it more of a vegetarian main course.

Make the pickled shallots · Put the sugar in a heavy-based pan with the vinegar, water, olive oil, garlic and thyme. Bring to the boil, then add the shallots and cook for 1 minute, then remove from the heat and leave to cool. Transfer to a jar and drain to use as required.

Blanch the beans · Trim the beans, keeping the pointy ends. Bring a large pan of water to the boil with 2 tablespoons of salt. Add the beans and cook for 4 minutes. Drain into a colander in the sink and quickly refresh under cold running water. Dry on kitchen paper.

Prepare the peaches · Preheat the oven to 180°C (350°F/Gas Mark 4). Cut the peaches into quarters, removing the stones. Heat an ovenproof frying pan over a medium heat. Add the peaches and cook for a few minutes to allow the natural sugars to caramelise and colour, turning once. Sprinkle over the sugar and allow it to melt and caramelise. Drizzle over the water and flip the peach on to the skin side. Transfer to the oven and roast for 2 minutes, then remove and add a couple of spoonfuls of the vinaigrette to the pan, swirling to evenly combine. This might need a little water if it splits – it needs to look like a warm caramel dressing.

Time to serve · Add some of the dressing to the plate. Put the beans and rocket in a bowl and toss with the rest of the dressing. Add four or five of the pickled shallot rings to the plate, then some of the bean and rocket mixture. Scatter over the toasted almonds and add a few more spoons of the dressing.

DESSERTS

These desserts are some of my favourites – I love sweet things. Whether you fancy something quick, like a chocolate mousse, or you want more of a family-style dessert for sharing, you'll find it here, and all of the ingredients can be picked up from the supermarket. A delicious dessert is a great finish to any meal, whether on a relaxed summer's afternoon, during the midweek rush or on a slow winter's evening – and maybe you can get the kids involved in making it too!

HOMEMADE CARAMEL ICE CREAM

200g caster sugar
355ml cream
150g egg yolks
250ml milk
200g honeycomb trimmings
(optional – see page 45)
salted caramel butter sauce
(see page 250), to serve

SERVES 8-10

Unlike many other ice-cream recipes, there's no need for any special equipment here. The caramel will stabilise the cream and keep the texture soft in the freezer. If you want to go a step further, break up some of the honeycomb from page 45 and fold it through to make one of my favourite childhood desserts.

Make the caramel · Heat a heavy-based pan over a medium heat. Add half of the sugar and heat until it has dissolved. Increase the heat and continue to cook, without stirring, until the mixture has turned a deep amber caramel, just swirling the pan occasionally to ensure the mixture caramelises evenly. Remove from the heat and whisk in 80ml of the cream.

Make the custard · Whisk the egg yolks and the rest of the sugar in a large bowl for a few minutes, until the sugar is fully incorporated and the yolks are a pale yellow. Place the milk in a pan and heat until it is not quite simmering, then very slowly pour it into the egg-yolk mixture. Pour it back into a clean pan and heat gently, stirring continuously, until the custard will coat the back of a spatula. If you have a thermometer, it should read 82°C.

Make the ice cream · Remove the custard from the heat and pour it on top of the caramel, mixing well. In a separate bowl, whisk the remaining 275ml of cream until stiff peaks have formed. Put the caramel custard into a stand mixer with a whisk attachment and whisk until it is completely cold, then fold in the whipped cream. Pour into a 1 litre rigid plastic container with a lid. Stick in pieces of the honeycomb, if using (reserving a little for decoration), so it is evenly distributed. Freeze for at least 2–3 hours, or overnight is best. This will keep for 1–2 weeks.

Time to serve · When ready to serve, scoop out balls of the ice cream, then scatter over the rest of the honeycomb, crumbling it into smaller pieces, if using. Finish with a drizzle of salted caramel butter sauce.

STRAWBERRY AND CITRUS FRUIT TRIFLE

FOR THE BASE
2½ packets strawberry jelly
    (135g each)
600ml boiling water
2 oranges
200g strawberries, hulled and
    halved
5 mint leaves, cut into strips
1 vanilla pod, split and seeds
    scraped out
1 × 250g packet trifle sponges,
    cut into small squares

FOR THE LIME CURD
135g caster sugar
finely grated zest and juice
    of 4 limes, plus 1 extra for
    garnish
4 eggs
2 strawberry jelly cubes
190g butter, diced and at room
    temperature

FOR THE LEMON CREAM
125g mascarpone
250ml double cream
2 tsp vanilla extract
1 tbsp icing sugar
finely grated zest of 2 lemons,
    plus 1 extra for garnish

SERVES 8-10

This is perfect for when strawberries are at their best. I've used packet jelly here because it's so convenient. Once you've put it all together, you just need to give it a few hours to set in the fridge.

Make the jelly base · Cut the strawberry jelly into cubes, then put in a bowl and pour over the boiling water, stirring until melted. Leave to cool for ten minutes. Using a Microplane, zest one of the oranges into a bowl and stir in the strawberries and mint with half of the vanilla seeds. Stir into the cooled jelly. Arrange the trifle sponges in the bottom of a glass trifle dish, and pour over the jelly mix. Chill for at least 2 hours to set.

Make the lime curd · Place the sugar in a large bowl with the lime zest and juice and whisk to combine. Add the eggs and whisk again. Bring a large pan of water to a simmer on a medium-high heat, and once it has reached a soft boil, put the bowl with the lime mixture on top and whisk frequently for about 10 minutes, until it is thick enough to hold the mark of a whisk. If you have a thermometer, you can check the temperature – it should be 84°C (183°F). Remove from the heat and whisk in the strawberry jelly cubes with the butter, continuing to whisk until everything has dissolved. Leave to cool down, then carefully spoon over the jelly and sponge mixture. Return the trifle bowl to the fridge.

Make the lemon cream · Using an electric beater, whisk the mascarpone and cream in a large bowl with the other half of the vanilla seeds, vanilla extract, icing sugar and lemon zest. When it has reached stiff peaks, carefully dollop it over the set lime-curd layer of the trifle. This will keep for up to 2 days in the fridge.

Time to serve · Use the remaining orange, lemon and lime to decorate the top of the trifle by grating a little of the zest of each one on top with a Microplane. Bring the trifle to the table in all its glory.

BAKED RICE PUDDING WITH POACHED APRICOTS AND PISTACHIOS

600ml vanilla stock syrup (see page 254)

500g ripe apricots, halved and stones removed

800ml milk

340ml double cream

2 cinnamon sticks

1 bay leaf

2 pieces of pared lemon rind

1 vanilla pod, split in half

2 tsp vanilla extract

40g butter, plus extra for greasing

95g caster sugar

140g arborio rice

½ whole nutmeg

40g honey

1 tbsp cornflour

50g pistachios, roughly chopped

SERVES 6

I love this old school-style of rice pudding, but I've added some aromatics here just to give it a bit of spice. With the nuttiness of the pistachios and a little bit of the pouring cream, this is a perfect dessert for me. When apricots aren't in season you can use tinned ones.

Poach the apricots · Put the vanilla stock syrup into a pan and bring to the boil. Reduce the heat to low, add the apricots and poach for 2–3 minutes, or 4–5 minutes if they are very firm. Turn off the heat. Transfer the apricots and syrup to a large jar and keep in the fridge at least overnight or up to 1 week.

Infuse the milk mixture · Put the milk and cream in a pan with the cinnamon, bay leaf, lemon rind, vanilla pod and extract. Bring to a simmer, then remove from the heat before it comes to the boil. Cover with cling film and leave to infuse for 30 minutes.

Make the rice pudding · Preheat the oven to 170°C (325°F/Gas Mark 3). Pass the infused milk mixture through a fine sieve into a large measuring jug. Put the butter and sugar into a large bowl and pour in all but 200ml of the flavoured milk, mixing to combine. Grease a 26cm round ovenproof dish and add the rice. Stir in the mixture from the bowl and grate over a little of the nutmeg. Bake for 1 hour, until the rice is tender and the top is bubbling and catching around the edges.

Make the pouring cream · Meanwhile, add the 200ml of flavoured milk into a clean pan and add the honey. Stir a little of the liquid into the cornflour in a small bowl, mixing with a spoon until smooth, and then pour back into the pan. Whisk well to combine, then put on a low heat and bring to a gentle simmer, whisking continuously. Cook for another 2–3 minutes, until thickened and smooth, stirring occasionally to ensure it does not stick to the bottom of the pan. Set aside.

Time to serve · Once the rice pudding is cooked, leave it to cool slightly. Meanwhile, gently warm the pouring cream through. Scoop the warm rice pudding into bowls and add some of the poached apricots. Lightly toast the pistachios in a frying pan, then roughly chop and scatter on top. Finish by pouring a little of the pouring cream around.

PERFECT CHOCOLATE MOUSSE

180g dark chocolate (at least
   70% cocoa solids)
70g milk chocolate
150ml cream
80ml milk
3 eggs, separated
20g caster sugar
200–300ml caramel chocolate
   sauce (optional – see page
   252)
300–400ml cream
grated chocolate, to decorate

SERVES 4–6

**This is my go-to recipe for chocolate mousse at home. It's perfect on
its own, but sometimes I whip a little bit of fresh cream for the top.**

Make the chocolate base · Break both chocolates into pieces, if necessary,
and put into a large heatproof bowl set over a pan of simmering water to melt,
stirring occasionally, then remove from the heat. Heat the cream and milk in a
separate small pan and bring to a simmer; just before it boils, remove from the
heat and whisk it into the melted chocolate with the egg yolks. Leave to cool
a little.

Make the mousse · Whisk the egg whites in a large bowl to soft peaks,
then scatter in the sugar and whisk again for about 30 seconds, until stiff
peaks form. Add a third of the egg white to the melted chocolate and mix
vigorously, working fast so the chocolate does not cool and harden. Then
carefully fold in the remaining egg whites using a large metal spoon or
spatula. Put a layer of the caramel chocolate sauce into each glass, if using,
and spoon the chocolate mousse on top. Leave to set in the fridge for 2–3
hours.

Time to serve · Whip the cream in a bowl until soft peaks form, add a couple
of spoonfuls to each glass, then scatter over the grated chocolate to decorate.

SPICED POACHED PEAR PUFF PASTRY WITH CATALAN CUSTARD

1 litre vanilla stock syrup (page 254)
4 star anise
40g fresh root ginger, sliced
4 whole cloves
1 cinnamon stick
4 ripe Conference pears
200g frozen puff pastry, thawed (preferably all butter)
a little plain flour, for dusting
1 egg, beaten with 1 tbsp water (egg wash)
4 tsp light brown sugar

FOR THE CATALAN CUSTARD

300ml cream
300ml milk
pared rind from 1 lemon
pared rind from 1 orange
5 green cardamon pods, cracked
2 star anise
1 tsp fennel seeds
5 egg yolks
100g caster sugar
1 tsp cornflour

SERVES 4

Once you've poached the pears in the spiced stock syrup, you can get your little ones involved in rolling the pastry around them. The Catalan custard can be made beforehand, and this dessert can be served hot or cold.

Poach the pears · Put the vanilla stock syrup into a pan with the star anise, ginger, cloves and cinnamon and bring to the boil. Peel the pears but keep the stalks intact. Reduce the heat to low, add the pears and bring back to the boil, then remove from the heat. Cover with parchment paper and put in the fridge for 1 hour.

Infuse the cream for the custard · Place the cream and milk in a pan with the lemon and orange rind, cardamon, star anise and fennel seeds. Bring to a simmer, then remove from the heat before it comes to the boil.

Make the custard · Whisk the egg yolks, sugar and cornflour in a large bowl and gradually pour in the infused cream mixture, whisking constantly. Pour the contents of the bowl into the pan and heat gently, stirring with a wooden spoon, until the custard is thickened and coats the back of the spoon but before any lumps form. Pass through a sieve into a jug. Cover with cling film against the surface of the custard to prevent a skin forming. Chill until needed.

Finish the pears · Preheat the oven to 210°C (410°F/Gas Mark 7). Roll out the pastry on a lightly floured board to a 3mm thickness. Cut off 4 × 20–25cm strips, 1cm wide, brush lightly with egg wash and dust with brown sugar, keeping away from the edges or it will not rise properly. Drain the pears and pat dry with kitchen paper, then gently trim their bottoms if they cannot stand up on their own. Carefully wrap a piece of the pastry around each one, tucking it underneath, and put them on a sturdy non-stick baking tray. Bake for 10 minutes, until the pastry is puffed up and golden and the pears are warmed through.

Time to serve · Put the spiced poached pears with puff pastry on plates and pour around warm or cold Catalan custard to serve.

ORANGE CRÈME BRÛLÉE

1 vanilla pod
300ml cream
1 tsp vanilla extract
2 oranges (or mandarins)
4 egg yolks
45g caster sugar
2 tbsp light brown sugar

SERVES 4

This is a classic. The zest gives it just the hit of orange it needs, and if you're making it for adults, you can add a half-shot of Cointreau to the mix. Cook it to a wobble, let it set in the fridge, then use a good blowtorch or really hot grill to give it that thick caramel top.

Flavour the cream · Lay the vanilla pod on a chopping board and slice lengthways through the middle with a sharp knife to split into two. Use the tip of a knife or a small teaspoon to scrape out all the tiny seeds, and put them into a small pan with the cream, adding the pod as well and the vanilla extract. Using a Microplane, grate in the orange zest. Bring the cream to a simmer, then remove from the heat before it comes to the boil.

Make the custard base · Meanwhile, whisk the egg yolks and caster sugar in a large bowl for 1 minute. Pour in the flavoured cream, stirring with the whisk and making sure you use a spatula to get all the vanilla seeds out of the bottom of the pan. Pour the custard into a large jug. Scoop off all the pale foam sitting on top of the liquid and discard, then give it another stir.

Bake the crème brûlées · Preheat the oven to 140°C (275°F/Gas Mark 1). Sit four 100ml ramekins in a shallow roasting tin. Pour enough hot water from the tap into the roasting tin so that it comes halfway up the sides of the ramekins. Pour the hot custard into the ramekins to fill them right up to the top. Bake for about 1 hour, checking regularly after 30 minutes, until the mixture is softly set. They should wobble a bit like jelly in the middle – it is important not to let them get too firm.

Cool down the crème brûlées · Carefully lift the ramekins out of the roasting tin on to a wire rack and leave them to cool for a couple of minutes, then put them in the fridge to cool completely.

Finish the dish · When you're ready to serve, wipe the top edge of the ramekins and sprinkle each one with about 1½ teaspoons of the sugar and gently roll it around for a thin even layer. Use a blowtorch to caramelise the sugar – simply hold the flame just above the sugar and keep moving it round and round until it's evenly caramelised. If you're using a grill, make sure it's really hot and flash the brûlées under it for about 30 seconds. Cut four slices from one of the oranges, remove all the pith and peel, then use them to decorate the brûlées to serve.

CROISSANT BREAD AND BUTTER PUDDING

200ml milk
350ml cream
1 vanilla pod, cut in half and
    seeds scraped out
3 eggs, plus 1 yolk
50g caster sugar
1 tsp vanilla extract
6 large croissants (day old is
    perfect)
200g granulated sugar
60ml water
140g Seville orange
    marmalade
75g raisins

FOR THE GLAZED PECANS
100g pecans
4 tbsp granulated sugar
4 tsp water

**FOR THE THYME, LEMON
AND HONEY CUSTARD**
300ml cream
300ml milk
2 tbsp honey
4 fresh thyme sprigs
2 pieces pared lemon rind
100g egg yolks (about 5 eggs)
50g caster sugar

SERVES 4-6

The butteriness of the croissants adds richness to this recipe, and the caramelised pecans and thick dusting of caramel make it even more luxurious.

Make the pudding mix · Preheat the oven to 150°C (300°F/Gas Mark 2). Put the milk, cream, vanilla pod and seeds in a pan and heat to just below boiling point. Whisk the eggs, yolk and caster sugar in a bowl until combined. Pour in the warm milk mixture, stirring constantly until smooth. Stir in the vanilla extract and set aside.

Prepare the croissants · Cut the croissants into 2cm slices and arrange in a single layer on a baking sheet. Bake for 5–10 minutes until crispy and golden.

Make the caramel powder · Put the granulated sugar and water into a heavy-based pan over a low heat until dissolved. Increase the heat and simmer until it turns to a dark caramel colour. Carefully pour the hot caramel over a silicone baking mat and leave to cool. When cold, break the caramel into pieces, put them into a coffee grinder or blender, and blitz to a powder.

Make the glazed pecans · Put the pecans, sugar and water into a heavy-based pan over a low heat, stirring until the sugar has dissolved. Increase the heat and keep mixing the nuts until they're glazed – 5–8 minutes. Tip on to a silicone mat and spread out to cool completely.

Finish the pudding · Lightly butter a 24cm × 17cm ovenproof dish. Spread both sides of the croissant slices with the marmalade, and use half the slices to cover the bottom of the dish in an overlapping layer. Pour over half of the pudding mix, discarding the vanilla pod, and then scatter over half the glazed pecans and raisins. Repeat these layers and leave to soak for 10–15 minutes.

Bake the pudding · Put the pudding dish into a large roasting tin and pour in enough hot water to come halfway up the sides. Bake at 160°C for 30–35 minutes, until lightly golden but with a slight wobble. Remove from the oven, sprinkle over an even layer of the caramel powder, and bake for another 3–5 minutes.

Make the thyme, lemon and honey custard · Meanwhile, heat the cream and milk with the honey, thyme and lemon rind in a pan over a medium heat, stirring until the honey has dissolved. Bring to the boil, then take off the heat, cover with cling film and leave to infuse for 10 minutes. Then put the egg yolks and sugar in a bowl and whisk in the infused milk. Pour this back into the pan and cook for a few minutes, until the custard has thickened and coats the back of a wooden spoon. Strain into a jug.

Time to serve · Serve the pudding straight to the table with the custard.

KNICKERBOCKER GLORY WITH POACHED FRUIT AND GINGER CAKE

FOR THE GINGER CAKE

115g butter, at room
   temperature
115g caster sugar
1 egg
325g black treacle
350g plain flour
2 tsp bicarbonate of soda
1 tsp salt
1 tsp ground cinnamon
1 tsp ground ginger
1 heaped tsp freshly grated
   root ginger
235ml hot water

FOR THE FRUIT AND JELLY

3 red plums (170g)
350ml vanilla stock syrup
   (page 254)
100ml water
50ml Ribena
125g blackberries
12g packet powdered gelatine
juice of 1 lemon

FOR THE WHITE
CHOCOLATE CHANTILLY

30g white chocolate, drops or
   broken into squares
10ml milk
260ml cream
20g sugar

TO FINISH

500ml tub vanilla ice cream

SERVES 4–6

🍞🍞🍞

This was a rare treat when I was a kid, and from memory it was fruit, jelly and ice cream. I've added a little twist here. If you make them in tall glasses, they can be shared – although it might cause a fight.

Make the ginger cake · Preheat the oven to 175°C (345°F/Gas Mark 3½). Put the butter and sugar into a stand mixer and cream together until light and fluffy. Add the egg and treacle and mix again, then add the flour, bicarbonate of soda, salt, cinnamon, ground and grated ginger and mix well again to combine. Pour in the hot water and mix to a dough. Line a 30cm × 20cm baking tin with parchment paper and pour in the ginger cake mixture, spreading it out evenly right to the edges of the tin. Bake for 30 minutes until well risen and slightly coming away from the sides. Leave to cool completely in the tin, then once cold break 175g of it into 1cm chunks. The leftover ginger cake can be eaten as a snack or frozen. Alternatively, you can crumble it and fold it through ice cream.

Poach the fruit · Cut the plums into quarters, removing the stones. Put the vanilla stock syrup into a large pan with the water and Ribena. Bring to the boil, then remove from the heat and add the plums and blackberries. Leave to cool down, then cover with a lid and chill for 1 hour.

Make the jelly · Once the fruit is ready, set a large sieve over a pan and carefully pour the fruit in to strain out the syrup. Transfer the poached fruit into a bowl and set aside. Put the syrup on a medium heat and bring to the boil, then add the gelatine powder and lemon juice and whisk well to combine. Pour into a bowl and leave to cool, then put in the fridge for at least 2 hours to set.

Make the Chantilly · Put the chocolate in a pan over a low heat with the milk, cream and sugar and whisk until the sugar has dissolved and the chocolate has melted. Remove from the heat and leave to cool, then chill in the fridge for 30 minutes to 1 hour until cold, then whisk until you have achieved medium peaks. Cover and chill until needed.

Time to serve · Spoon the poached blackberries and plums into the bottom of knickerbocker glory glasses. Add one spoon of the set jelly and then divide the white chocolate Chantilly among them. Add a scoop of vanilla ice cream to each one and top with a layer of the broken ginger cake. Repeat the layers another time and serve immediately.

BREADS

Making bread is a skill developed with experience. I've learned some of these recipes through my years working in top kitchens, and here I've picked the simpler, more approachable ones that are versatile enough to use for different things. All you need is a little patience to let it prove and a hot oven and you can't go wrong. Starting a meal with some warm homemade bread is one of the great joys of life.

HONEY ROAST GARLIC, ROSEMARY AND TOMATO FOCACCIA

STARTER
22.5g dried yeast (or 45g fresh)
15g caster sugar
180ml lukewarm water
225g Tipo '00' flour

FOCACCIA
455g Tipo '00' flour
400g plain flour, plus extra for dusting
45g sugar
13g salt
220ml extra virgin olive oil, plus extra for greasing and drizzling
490ml water

TOPPINGS
100g cherry tomatoes, halved
handful fresh rosemary sprigs
100g honey roast garlic (page 235)
½ tsp sea salt flakes

SERVES 8–12

Warm focaccia is so good – just serve with some olive oil for dipping. This bread works well with all of the soups in this book.

Make the starter · First, make the starter. Stir the yeast with the sugar and four tablespoons of the warm water. Let it stand for 10 minutes, then add the rest of the warm water. Transfer to the bowl of a stand mixer with a dough hook attached and, on the lowest setting, gradually add the flour. Once it's a wet dough, transfer to a well-oiled bowl, cover with a wet tea towel and leave for 20 minutes to prove.

Make the dough · Put both the flours for the focaccia in the cleaned bowl of the stand mixer, with dough hook attached, and add the sugar, salt and olive oil. Pour in the water and then add the starter. Mix at a medium to low speed for 5 minutes, until it comes together in a slightly sticky dough.

Knead the dough · Tip the dough out on to a lightly floured work surface, scraping around the sides of the bowl. Knead for about 5 minutes, until the dough is soft and less sticky, then put in a clean bowl, cover with a tea towel and leave to prove at room temperature for 1 hour, until doubled in size.

Shape the focaccia · Generously oil a shallow rectangular baking tin (about 20cm × 30cm). Tip the dough into the tin, then use your hands to stretch it out until it reaches the corners of the tin. Cover with a clean wet towel and leave to prove at room temperature for another 35 minutes.

Cook the focaccia · Preheat the oven to 180°C (350°F/Gas Mark 4). Tip the tomatoes into a bowl and toss with about a tablespoon of olive oil. Press the dough with your fingers to make dimples and add the tomatoes and push in the rosemary and garlic. Scatter over the sea salt and bake for 40 minutes until deep golden and puffed up. While the focaccia is still hot, drizzle over another tablespoon of oil. Leave to cool completely in the tin.

Time to serve · Cut the focaccia into slices or squares and use as required. It will keep wrapped or in an airtight container for up to 2 days.

GREEN OLIVE CIABATTA

5g dried yeast (or 10g fresh)
600ml warm water
800g plain flour, plus extra for
 dusting
16g salt
100g stoned green olives,
 finely chopped
50ml extra virgin olive oil

MAKES THREE LOAVES

This is such a great bread and so simple – you really just need the patience to do the turns. A lot of dusting will make the dough easier to work with. Good ciabatta is pale in colour, and the heavy flour on top blisters as it cooks.

Make the dough · Combine the yeast and warm water in a jug to dissolve. Put the flour, salt and olives in a large bowl and make a well in the middle. Pour in the yeast mixture and combine with your hand, gradually incorporating the flour. (It will be a very wet dough.) Pour a little of the olive oil onto the dough. Grab one of the corners of the dough and fold it into the middle, turn the bowl, and then repeat with three more corners of the dough until it's a rough ball shape. Cover with cling film. Leave to prove for 35–40 minutes at room temperature.

Shape the dough · After the dough has doubled, fold it inwards on itself again, as above, to make a ball, then cover it again with the cling film and leave to prove for another 35 minutes. Repeat this process another 2 times.

Cook the dough · Preheat the oven to 210°C (410°F/Gas Mark 6). Tip the dough on to a well-floured surface and dust heavily with more flour. Using a knife or pastry-scraper, divide the dough in three. Shape each piece of dough into a 30cm × 10–12cm rectangle. Dust again with more flour. Transfer each loaf to a well-floured baking sheet, then allow to rest for another 10 minutes. Bake for 20 minutes, until the flour has blistered and a small sharp knife comes out clean. Move to a wire rack and leave to cool for 1 hour.

Time to serve · Slice the ciabatta and serve with tomato salad (see page 146).

BURGER BUNS

80ml milk
200ml water
500g plain flour, plus extra for
  dusting
12.5g dried yeast (or use 25g
  fresh)
10g salt
25g caster sugar
1 egg, plus extra yolk for
  glazing
30g butter
vegetable oil, for greasing
1 heaped tbsp sesame seeds

MAKES 10

This is a good, solid recipe, perfect with any of the burgers in this book. Although we feel it works better with fresh yeast, dried yeast will do.

Prepare the liquids · In a small pan, gently heat the milk and water until warm but not hot (30°C/85°F).

Assemble the dough · Tip the flour, yeast, salt, sugar and egg into the bowl of a stand mixer with a dough hook attached. Pour over the warm milk mixture, then mix at medium speed until it comes together as a shaggy dough. Add the butter to the dough and mix for about 4–5 minutes, until it becomes tighter and springy. Shape the dough into a ball and put in a clean, oiled bowl. Cover with cling film and leave in the fridge for 2 hours or until doubled in size.

Shape the burger buns · Tip the dough onto a lightly floured surface and roll into a long sausage shape. Halve the dough, then divide each half into five pieces, so you have ten equal-sized portions – each should weigh about 80g. Roll each into a tight ball and put on to two parchment-lined baking trays, leaving some room between each ball for rising. Cover with a damp tea towel and leave in a warm place for about 1 hour or until almost doubled in size.

Time to cook · Preheat the oven to 200°C (400°F/Gas Mark 6). When the dough balls are ready, lightly glaze each one with the egg yolk beaten with a little extra water and scatter over the sesame seeds. Bake for 12 minutes until light brown and hollow sounding when tapped on the base. Leave to cool on a wire rack and use as required. They'll keep for 2 days in an airtight container at room temperature and up to 3 months in the freezer.

PARMESAN AND SEMOLINA BREAD

250ml water

60g milk

2 tsp honey

360g fine semolina flour, plus extra for sprinkling

140g strong white bread flour, plus extra for dusting

8g dried yeast (or 16g fresh yeast)

15g salt

50g freshly grated Parmesan, plus a little extra

vegetable oil, for brushing

MAKES 1 LOAF OR 6 MINI LOAVES

This recipe reminds me of being a young chef learning how to make bread in London. The semolina gives a really nice texture, and the cheesy flavour works with most soups.

Prepare the liquids · In a small pan, gently heat the water, milk and honey until warm but not hot (30°C/85°F).

Assemble the dough · Tip the semolina, flour, yeast and salt into the bowl of a stand mixer with a dough hook attached. Pour over the warm water mixture, then mix until it comes together as a shaggy dough. Add the Parmesan and mix for 5 minutes. Remove the dough from the mixer, shape into a ball and put into a clean, oiled bowl. Cover with cling film and leave at room temperature for 1 hour, or until doubled in size.

Shape the dough · Tip the dough onto a lightly floured surface and shape it into an oblong loaf. Brush a 900g loaf tin or 6 mini loaf tins with vegetable oil and sprinkle with semolina. Add the dough to the tin (divide and shape the dough accordingly if using the mini loaf tins), and place on to a baking tray. Scatter a little extra Parmesan on top and add a light sprinkling of semolina. Cover with a damp tea towel and leave in a warm place for 10 minutes.

Time to cook · Preheat the oven to 200°C (400°F/Gas Mark 6). Bake for 12–14 minutes for the mini loaves and 35–40 minutes for a large loaf or until a small sharp knife comes out clean. Leave to cool on a wire rack and serve hot with butter.

FLATBREADS WITH COCONUT AND CORIANDER AND ROSEMARY AND GARLIC

290ml lukewarm water

14g dried yeast (28g fresh yeast)

500g plain flour, plus extra for dusting

10g caster sugar

20g salt

1 tbsp toasted desiccated coconut

1 tbsp fresh rosemary leaves

1 tbsp chopped fresh coriander

1 thinly sliced garlic (on a Microplane)

extra virgin olive oil, for brushing

**MAKES ABOUT
10 FLATBREADS**

There are two flavour choices here, depending on the curry you want these to accompany. This recipe is a fun one, because it puffs up full of air in the pan – give it a go and see.

Make the dough · Mix the lukewarm water with the yeast in a jug and set aside. Sieve the flour into a large bowl with the sugar and salt, make a well in the centre and mix in the yeast mixture until it comes together. Turn out of bowl and knead lightly for 5 minutes.

Flavour the dough · Split the dough in half and fold the coconut and rosemary into one piece and the coriander and garlic into the other. On a floured work surface, knead each dough again for 5 minutes, until you have a smooth and elastic dough. Put each dough into a clean bowl and cover with cling film. Set aside for about 2 hours or until doubled in size.

Shape the dough · Gently remove the doughs from the bowls and divide into 80g balls. Working with a floured rolling pin, roll each ball out to a circle about 5mm thick. Arrange on damp tea towels dusted with flour and cover with more damp tea towels dusted with flour. Leave for another 50 minutes to prove.

Cook the flatbreads · Preheat a large non-stick frying pan or flat griddle pan over a medium to high heat. Once the pan is warm, add one of the flatbreads, and turn every 20–30 seconds until puffed up and golden. Lightly brush with the oil, then place to one side and keep warm while you cook the remainder. Serve immediately.

JARS

These jars are an important part of this cookbook – they're the building blocks of many of the recipes. Some of them are super easy and some take a little more effort, but all of them could become staple elements of your home cooking. I've used many of these in restaurants over the years, and some I've learned from other chefs over the course of my career, but I use all of them in my own home cooking. Professional kitchens are built on these kinds of trustworthy recipes that can be relied on to produce consistent results. Here, I've tried to adapt that idea for the home cook, always keeping in mind the challenges of a domestic kitchen. Many of the jars have a decent shelf life, so you can get the maximum results from making the effort to cook and store them, and many can also be frozen. So why not invest in some storage jars and get to work, and you'll soon be enjoying the fruits of your labour.

SHALLOT REDUCTION

4 tsp olive oil
240g shallots, sliced
3 garlic cloves, peeled
1 fresh thyme sprig
1 bay leaf
5 black peppercorns
100ml white wine vinegar
100ml dry white wine
pinch of salt

MAKES ABOUT 300ML

Make this up and store it in your fridge. It will keep for weeks, and you can use it as a base for all butter sauces – hollandaise, Béarnaise or the mustard butter sauce in this book (see page 15). It adds depth to sauces and the flavour lasts longer in the mouth – it's the balance of the acidity with the butter that makes it a success.

Make the shallot reduction · Heat the oil in a heavy-based pan over a medium to low heat, and sauté the shallots, garlic, thyme, bay leaf and peppercorns for 8–10 minutes, until softened and translucent with no colour. Pour in the vinegar and wine and season with salt, then increase the heat and reduce by half. Leave to cool, then pour into a jar. This will keep for up to 2 months in the fridge. Pass through a sieve to use as required.

ROAST CHICKEN-WING GRAVY

750g chicken wings
200ml vegetable oil
250g carrots, cut into chunks
50g garlic, separated into
    cloves and peeled
50g butter
1 onion, roughly chopped
200g celery, chopped
4 fresh thyme sprigs
4 bay leaves
150ml water
1.5 litres chicken stock (made
    with 2 chicken jelly stock
    pots)
15 white peppercorns

MAKES 400-500ML

Simply roast the chicken wings in the oven, then colour the veg, bring it to a simmer and reduce. Having some of this in the freezer will make a Sunday roast dinner – or even Christmas dinner – much easier. It's a great quick fix, as the wings give a naturally sweet roasted flavour.

Roast the chicken wings · Preheat the oven to 180°C (350°F/Gas Mark 4). Using a large sharp knife, cut the chicken wings in half and spread out in a large roasting tin. Roast for 30–35 minutes, until cooked through and golden brown.

Make the gravy base · Heat the oil in a large pan over a medium-high heat. Add the carrots and garlic and sauté for 8–10 minutes, then add the butter and tip in the onion, celery and herbs and sauté for another 6–8 minutes. Stir in the roasted chicken wings and deglaze the pan with 150ml of water. Transfer to a colander set over a large bowl and drain off the excess fat.

Cook the gravy · Return the drained chicken wings and vegetables to the pan and add the stock and peppercorns. Bring to the boil and then reduce the heat and simmer for 1 hour and 20 minutes until reduced by half.

Finish the gravy · Strain the gravy through a fine sieve into a clean smaller pan, and then simmer again to reduce until you have a well-flavoured gravy.

Store the gravy · Pour the gravy into a jar and store in the fridge for up to 3 days, reheating to use as required. Alternatively, pour into a suitable container and freeze for up to 3 months. You can use this to make great onion gravy by adding some soft onions with thyme, bay leaf and garlic (see page 231) or use for your turkey Christmas dinner.

BÉCHAMEL SAUCE

1 litre milk
2 garlic cloves, peeled
2 fresh thyme sprigs
2 bay leaves
50g butter
50g plain flour
pinch of ground nutmeg
salt and freshly ground white
    pepper

MAKES ABOUT 1 LITRE

This is another classic made simpler for dads at home. It's perfect on a pizza, or you can stir a little pasta through it with some cheese, or you could add parsley and serve it with ham. On a Sunday, add a couple of handfuls of cheese and serve it with your cauliflower.

Infuse the milk · Pour the milk into a heavy-based pan over a low heat and add the garlic, thyme and bay leaves. Bring to a bare simmer, then switch off the heat and leave to infuse for 20 minutes. Strain into a jug, discarding the garlic and herbs.

Make the roux · Wipe the pan clean and return to a medium heat. Melt the butter and then stir in the flour until smooth. Cook for 1 minute, until the mixture turns a light golden colour, stirring continuously.

Finish the sauce · Increase the heat to medium-high and slowly whisk in the infused liquid until thickened. Bring to the boil, then reduce the heat to its lowest setting and simmer for 6–8 minutes, until smooth. Add the nutmeg and season with salt and pepper. Pour into a jar and chill in the fridge for 4–5 days, or freeze in suitable containers. Use as required.

BASIL PESTO

50g pine nuts
150ml olive oil
50g freshly grated Parmesan
  cheese
70g fresh basil leaves
1 garlic clove, peeled
1 tbsp flaky salt
½ tsp cracked black pepper

MAKES ABOUT 300G

This version of the classic is nice and chunky and not oily. You can use it for so many things – salads, pastas or even just with some crusty bread for dipping.

Prepare the nuts · Preheat the oven to 180°C (350°F/Gas Mark 4). Spread the pine nuts out on a small baking sheet and toast in the oven for 5 minutes. Pour the oil into the metal blending bowl of a food processor or blender with the cheese and roasted nuts. Chill in the freezer for 30 minutes.

Make the pesto · Add the 70g basil leaves to the bowl with the garlic and pulse for 5 seconds at a time until blitzed but still chunky – do not purée it. Season with salt and pepper and transfer to a clean jar or container. This will keep in the fridge for up to 1 week.

FRESH HERB SALSA VERDE

50g fresh tarragon leaves
50g flat-leaf parsley leaves
40g baby capers
1 garlic clove, peeled
3 tsp Dijon mustard
2 tbsp sherry vinegar
200ml extra virgin olive oil
sea salt and freshly ground
   black pepper

MAKES ABOUT 300ML

Get some herbs from the supermarket and try this simple salsa verde. It's perfect with meat or fish or even sprinkled on some hot new potatoes. It's a staple in most kitchens and at the barbecue.

Make the salsa verde · Finely chop the tarragon and parsley leaves, then put them in a large bowl. Rinse the capers and drain on kitchen paper, then finely chop and add to the bowl. Using a mandolin or very sharp knife, cut the garlic into wafer-thin slices and add to the bowl. Whisk in the Dijon mustard, sherry vinegar and olive oil. Season to taste and transfer to a clean jar. This will keep for up to 2 weeks in the fridge – use as required.

FRESH HERB GREEN CHIMICHURRI

300ml olive oil
4 garlic cloves, chopped
10 fresh thyme sprigs
8 fresh rosemary sprigs
50g fresh chives
50g flat-leaf parsley
50g fresh coriander
finely grated zest and juice of
    1 lemon
1 banana shallot, finely
    chopped
½ long red chilli, deseeded and
    diced
10g dried oregano
10g red wine vinegar
sea salt flakes and freshly
    ground black pepper

MAKES ABOUT 500G JAR

This is a good, versatile sauce to accompany most meats, particularly beef. No sticky sauces here! The fresh herbs are easily sourced in the supermarket. The vinegar and chilli bring a little bit of tangy heat.

Make the herb oil · Heat a large heavy-based pan over a medium heat. Pour in the oil and add the garlic, thyme and rosemary. Reduce the heat to low and cook for 10 minutes to infuse the herbs into the oil. Remove the thyme and rosemary and leave to cool.

Make the chimichurri · Meanwhile, roughly chop the chives and place in a blender. Pick the leaves from the parsley and coriander and add those as well. Add the lemon zest and juice, then pour in the oil and pulse until you have a coarse sauce. Using a spatula, transfer to a bowl. Stir in the shallot, chilli, oregano and vinegar until evenly combined. Season to taste and pour into clean jars. I recommend that you use this straightaway, but it will store in the fridge for up to 1 week. Use as required.

TEMPURA BATTER

150g plain flour
150g cornflour
1 tsp baking powder
½ tsp bicarbonate of soda
450ml cold sparkling water

MAKES ABOUT 750ML

This is the trusty tempura batter mix I've used for years. It's not too thick, so the crispiness just coats and no more. Add the sparkling water when you are ready to use it. You could store the dry ingredients in a jar, and it will keep for about three months in the cupboard.

Make the batter · Place the plain flour, cornflour, baking powder and bicarbonate of soda in a large bowl and whisk in the sparkling water. This is best used immediately but will last for up to 15 minutes once the water has been added.

BEER AND VODKA BATTER

200g rice flour
105g self-raising flour
1 tsp baking powder
1 tsp honey
170ml cold vodka
275ml cold beer

MAKES ABOUT 750ML

This batter is a little more pricey but so worth it. Be precise here – weigh it exactly to the gram. Whatever you're frying – fish, vegetables or even sausages – you'll need to flour them first and cook at about 155–160°C (310–320°F) so the boiling oil doesn't blow the batter off. It is literally that light but also so, so crispy – enjoy! This will be enough for two or three pieces of fish, so you might need double the batter if cooking. It's important that you only add the liquids to the dry mix just before cooking.

Make the batter · Place the rice flour, self-raising flour and baking powder in a large bowl. When ready to cook, stir the honey into the vodka in a large jug until dissolved. Pour in the beer and then whisk the liquids into the flour mixture until nice and shiny – the texture should be like semi-whipped double cream, which means it will easily stick to anything you are coating.

PIZZA TOMATO SAUCE

4 tsp olive oil
1 small onion, diced
2 garlic cloves thinly sliced
½ mild red chilli, deseeded and
  finely chopped
½ tsp dried oregano
400g tin San Marzano whole
  peeled plum tomatoes
2 tsp salt
1 tbsp sugar
10g fresh basil leaves, finely
  chopped

MAKES ABOUT 500ML

Everyone needs a good tomato sauce, and this is perfect for pizza. I like this recipe because the tomatoes aren't cooked - you simply crush them with your hands. Once it's made it can be frozen, and you can also use it with pasta and topped with some cheese as a quick dinner for the kids

Make the sauce ▪ Heat the oil in a heavy-based pan over a medium heat. Sauté the onion and garlic for 2–3 minutes, until softened and transparent. Stir in the chilli and oregano and cook for another 30 seconds. Remove from the heat and break the tomatoes with your hands as you add them from the tin. Add the salt, sugar and basil, then blitz with a hand blender until smooth. Pour into a clean jar. This will keep in the fridge for a week.

BARBECUE GLAZE

300ml pineapple juice (fresh
    for best results)
300ml apple juice
160g ketchup
100ml cider vinegar
80g honey
80g light brown sugar
55g light soy sauce
50g Worcestershire sauce
40g Frank's hot sauce
25g barbecue spice rub (page
    228)
20g English mustard

MAKES 1 LITRE

**This might well become your go-to sauce for outside cooking – you'll
find yourself using it again and again. It's quick to prepare and a little
spicy. If you can get your hands on a juicer, I strongly recommend using
fresh pineapple juice for this recipe – it has great flavour – but if not,
pineapple juice from a carton will work just fine.**

Prepare the glaze · Place all the ingredients in a heavy-based pan and bring
to the boil, stirring until the sugar has dissolved. Leave to cool a little, then
transfer to a jar and store in the fridge for up to 1 week. Use as required.

HOMEMADE BARBECUE SAUCE

100ml olive oil
20g shallot, sliced
75g garlic cloves, peeled and
   thinly sliced
85g fresh root ginger, peeled
   and sliced
5 bay leaves
40g mild Madras curry powder
30g Thai red curry paste
65g English mustard
8g smoked paprika
130ml rice wine vinegar
140ml light soy sauce
85ml Worcestershire sauce
450g tomato ketchup
60g black treacle
70g honey
150g dark brown sugar
140g lemon juice
150ml water

MAKES ABOUT 1.5 LITRES

There are a good few ingredients to gather here, but it's well worth the effort. Use a good blender, as the sauce needs to be super smooth.

Cook the aromatics · Heat the oil in a large pan over a medium heat and sauté the shallot for a few minutes until softened and transparent. Add the garlic, ginger and bay leaves and sauté for 3–5 minutes without colouring.

Make the sauce · Stir in the curry powder, red curry paste, mustard and smoked paprika and sauté for another 5–7 minutes until the spices are cooked. Add the vinegar, soy, Worcestershire sauce and ketchup, stirring to combine, and reduce the heat. Add the treacle, honey and sugar, stirring to combine. Add the lemon juice and mix well. Pour in the water and bring to the boil, then reduce the heat to a slow simmer and cook for 5 minutes.

Finish the sauce · Remove the sauce from the heat, transfer to a blender, and blend until smooth. Then pass through a fine sieve into a bowl and leave to cool down completely, then put into jars. The flavour improves after 2 weeks, but it will keep for up to 1 month in the fridge.

BARBECUE SPICE RUB

2 tbsp salt
2 tbsp ground turmeric
2 tbsp paprika
2 tbsp onion powder
1 tsp sugar
1 tsp garlic powder
1 tsp dried chilli flakes
1 tsp cracked black pepper

MAKES 140G

Rub some of this into the meat 15 to 30 minutes before you barbecue. It's light enough that it doesn't overpower the meat but spicy enough to give you what you want from good barbecue. Don't be too heavy-handed, so it doesn't dominate the flavour of the meat, but it will help with the crust.

Prepare the spice rub · Place all the ingredients in a bowl and stir to combine, then transfer to a jar and store in the cupboard for up to 2 months. Using a sharp object, poke some holes in the top of the jar, and use as required.

HOMEMADE BROWN SAUCE

3 star anise
6 whole cloves
200ml cider vinegar
200ml water
200ml apple juice
100g black treacle
60g dark brown sugar
1 red onion, chopped
3 cooking apples, peeled, cored
and chopped
3 pears, peeled, cored and
chopped
300g dates, stones removed
and chopped
20g fresh root ginger, peeled
and chopped
1 red chilli, deseeded and
chopped
1 green chilli, chopped
100ml Worcestershire sauce
1 tsp ground ginger
1 tsp English mustard powder
1 tsp ground allspice

MAKES 700-800ML

Once you get all the ingredients together for this, the actual cooking is easy. You might be saying 'Just buy the brown sauce', but this will lift any dish to a new height. It makes a good gift for friends for birthdays or Christmas.

Infuse the liquid · Take a small piece of muslin or a brand new J-cloth, place the star anise and cloves in the middle and tie up securely with kitchen string. Put into a large heavy-based pan with the vinegar, water and apple juice. Bring to the boil, then remove from the heat and leave the spices to infuse in the liquid for 20 minutes.

Cook the sauce · Add the treacle and brown sugar to the infused liquid with the onion, apples, pears, dates, fresh ginger, chillies, Worcestershire sauce and spices. Bring to the boil, stirring to dissolve the sugar. Then reduce the heat to very low and cook for 50 minutes, stirring regularly to ensure it does not stick to the bottom.

Finish the sauce · Remove the muslin bag from the cooked-down mixture, transfer the mixture to a blender, and blend until smooth. Pass through a fine metal sieve on to a cold tray so that it cools quickly, and then spoon into a clean jar. Use as required. This will keep for 2–3 weeks in the fridge.

SOFT ONIONS WITH THYME, BAY LEAF AND GARLIC

100ml olive oil
100g butter
400g onions, thinly sliced
3 garlic cloves, peeled
4 bay leaves
4 fresh thyme sprigs
1 tsp sea salt flakes

MAKES 250G

This is a good base that can be made-up beforehand and added to many things. Put it on potatoes or pizzas or put spoonfuls of it into your gravy. It's subtly sweet and aromatic.

Cook the onions · Heat the oil and butter in a pan over a low heat. Once the butter has melted, add the onions, garlic, bay leaves, thyme and salt, stirring to combine and allowing it to sizzle. Cook gently for 10–15 minutes – you are cooking the onions really slowly, without colour, to bring out their natural sweetness. The onions should be soft and translucent. Remove from the heat and leave to cool down, then pack into a clean jar and store in the fridge for up to 1 week.

CARAMELISED ONION MARMALADE

100ml olive oil
4 large onions, sliced thinly on
 a mandolin (1.2kg)
3 garlic cloves, peeled
2 fresh thyme sprigs
150g butter, diced
150g Demerara sugar
100ml balsamic vinegar
20g salt

MAKES ABOUT 1KG

The trick here is to colour the onions first, then deglaze with the vinegar. This tastes great, adds dimensions of flavour and is something you can easily make at home and keep in the fridge. It can be used for so many things, and it's in a number of the recipes in this book.

Caramelise the onions · Heat a heavy-based pan over a low heat. Add the olive oil and then tip in the onions, garlic and thyme. Sauté for 10–15 minutes, until the onions are soft and transparent. Increase the heat and add all the butter. Continue to sauté for 10–12 minutes until the onions caramelise and turn dark in colour but aren't burnt, stirring occasionally.

Finish the onion marmalade · Once the onions have caramelised, tip them into a sieve or colander set over a bowl. Discard the drained-off fat. Return the onions to the pan and hit them with the sugar. Cook for 2 minutes, stirring until the sugar has dissolved. Stir the balsamic vinegar into the onion mixture, scraping the bottom of the pan to remove any sediment and allowing it to bubble down a little. Remove from the heat. Season to taste with the salt and leave to cool.

Store the onion marmalade · Spoon the onion marmalade into clean jars. Use as required. This will keep for up to 3 weeks in the fridge.

HONEY ROAST GARLIC

20 garlic cloves, peeled
50g olive oil
50g butter
2 fresh rosemary sprigs
3 tbsp honey
5g salt

MAKES 200G

This is quite versatile – it's boiled a few times to take down the fieriness of the garlic and has an extra dimension when caramelised with honey and butter. Outside of the recipes in this book, it can simply be spread on toasted sourdough or served with most meats.

Blanch the garlic · Put the garlic cloves into a pan and cover with cold water, then bring to the boil. Drain and repeat this process three times, which removes the strong flavour of the garlic. Drain well on kitchen paper and pat dry.

Cook the garlic · Heat the oil in a heavy-based frying pan over a medium heat. Add the garlic cloves and cook for 2–3 minutes, until they start to colour. Add butter and rosemary and continue to cook for 2–3 minutes until the butter turns nut-brown. Then add the honey and 3 tablespoons of water and stir with a rubber spatula, being careful not to break the garlic, until the mixture has emulsified. Season with salt, then leave to cool. Pack into a clean jar. This will keep for up to 1 month in the fridge.

CONFIT GARLIC

250ml vegetable oil
40 garlic cloves, peeled
3 fresh thyme sprigs

MAKES 400G

This stores really well and is roast garlic in its simplest form. Prepared this way, it can be added to so many dishes.

Make the confit · Put the oil in a heavy-based pan with the garlic and thyme. Bring to the boil, then turn the heat down, and as soon as the garlic is nicely golden remove it from the heat. Set aside for 40 minutes to 1 hour – it will continue to cook and soften in the warm oil. Transfer to a jar – this will keep for up to 2 weeks in the fridge.

KIMCHI

1 Chinese cabbage
1 mooli radish
2 tbsp sea salt flakes
135g caster sugar
20 garlic cloves, peeled
100g fresh root ginger, peeled
    and chopped
65g gochugaru (Korean chilli
    powder)
60ml Thai fish sauce (nam pla)
60ml light soy sauce
130ml water
2 tbsp salted shrimps
1 large carrot, peeled and
    julienned
4 spring onions, trimmed and
    finely shredded

MAKES ABOUT 1 LITRE

I love kimchi – not only is it super healthy, but it rewards patience, as the flavour gets better and better as it ages. There's no cooking – you just get the ingredients (most can be found in an Asian supermarket), get it made, and pop it up on a shelf out of the way to do its thing. If you like spice, this is perfect and it adds so much to many foods – it's particularly great with fish.

Brine the vegetables · Trim the cabbage and cut into 2.5cm chunks. Peel the mooli and cut into 1.5cm cubes. Place both in a colander and rinse well, then sprinkle over the salt and half of the sugar and toss until evenly combined. Set aside for 1 hour, then rinse again and dry thoroughly. Transfer to a large bowl.
Make the kimchi · Put the garlic, ginger, gochugaru, fish sauce, soy sauce, water, salted shrimps and the rest of the sugar into a blender and blitz to a smooth paste. Toss into the cabbage mixture with the carrot and spring onions. Pack into a large jar, seal and leave to ferment in a cool dry place for 3 days, then chill. This will reach its peak flavour in 2 weeks; it will last up to 3 months in the fridge, but it will get stronger in flavour.

PEAR AND SHALLOT CHUTNEY

80g olive oil
3 banana shallots, sliced
1 heaped tbsp diced root
   ginger
heaped ½ tsp ground
   cinnamon
½ tsp yellow mustard seeds
½ tsp English mustard powder
100g dark brown sugar
120ml cider vinegar
4 large firm ripe pears, peeled,
   quartered, cored and diced
4 tbsp golden raisins
150ml lemon juice

MAKES 500G

This chutney can be used with savoury breakfasts, to accompany steaks and meats or on the cheese board. You just get it all into a pot and cook it down to the right consistency. And with a bit of time, it starts to mature and taste better.

Make the reduction · Heat the oil in a heavy-based pan over a low heat. Add the shallots and ginger and sauté for about 5 minutes, until soft and transparent. Tip in the spices and cook for 1 minute, stirring. Stir in the sugar and vinegar and simmer until reduced by half, stirring occasionally to ensure the mixture does not stick to the bottom of the pan.

Finish the chutney · Add the pears to the reduced mixture with the raisins and cook on a slow simmer for an 1 hour and 15 minutes, stirring occasionally, until reduced by half again. Stir in the lemon juice, and transfer into clean jars and store in the fridge for up to 1 month. Use as required.

SPRING ONION AND GINGER RELISH

10–12 spring onions
1 large cucumber
10g sugar
1 tsp Maldon sea salt
20g sherry vinegar
25g light soy sauce
30g freshly grated root ginger
20g finely chopped white
    pickled ginger
10g fresh finely chopped
    chives
90g olive oil

MAKES 400G

Served cold, this is perfect for a barbecue. It's got a subtle freshness, as well as a sweetness and stickiness, that works great with grilled meats.

Prepare the vegetables · Trim the spring onions and very thinly slice the green parts – the whites can be reserved and used in another recipe. Cut the cucumber into quarters and cut away the seeds, then coarsely grate it using the largest side of a box grater. Squeeze a little with your hands to remove the excess moisture – you'll need 130g.

Make the relish · Put the sugar and salt into a bowl with the sherry vinegar and soy sauce. Stir until dissolved, then add the spring onions, cucumber, root and pickled ginger, chives and oil. Stir until evenly combined, then pour into a clean jar. Store in the fridge for up to 5 days.

TOMATO AND YELLOW PEPPER RELISH

3 yellow peppers, deseeded
    and diced
10 ripe tomatoes, diced
1 large onion, diced
1 garlic clove, grated
1 tsp freshly grated root ginger
250ml white wine vinegar
170g light brown sugar
1 bay leaf
1 tsp yellow mustard seeds
1 tsp fennel seeds
1 tsp ground allspice
½ tsp cumin seeds
1 tbsp salt

MAKES 1KG

This makes a great burger relish. It's better than shop-bought because it's fresher and it's cooked quicker. Once you taste it, you'll realise how many things it can go with.

Make the relish · Put the peppers, tomatoes, onion, garlic and ginger in a large pan over a medium heat. Add the vinegar, sugar, bay leaf, spices and salt and bring to the boil, stirring occasionally. Simmer for about 30 minutes, until the relish has developed a nice red colour and has reduced and thickened.

Time to serve · Pour the relish into clean jars and leave to cool, then seal with lids. This can be used immediately or will keep well for up to 6–8 weeks in the fridge.

LEMON, GARLIC AND TARRAGON DRESSING

5g salt
25g sugar
75ml lemon juice
75ml extra virgin olive oil
75ml olive oil (or pomace oil)
2 garlic cloves, crushed
2 fresh tarragon sprigs

MAKES 300ML

I always have a bottle of this lying around – it takes me back to my years in London. Its simple flavours come together in a light dressing that can be used all year round. The flavours of the whole tarragon sprigs and garlic cloves will develop beautifully over a week or so.

Make the dressing · Put all the ingredients in a screw-topped jar and shake vigorously until the dressing has emulsified.
Store the dressing · Chill the dressing until needed and use as required. This will keep for up to 3 weeks in the fridge.

ORANGE YOGHURT DRESSING

3 large oranges
25g sugar
20ml white wine vinegar
25ml water
200ml vegetable or oil
30g Greek strained yoghurt
juice of ½ lemon

MAKES 400ML

This is lovely if adding oranges to a salad. It's sweet and a little tart, which works well with peppery leaves like watercress and rocket, and it adds a freshness when served with raw shaved vegetables.

Prepare the orange syrup · Zest two oranges into a bowl. Zest half an orange into a separate bowl and set aside. Cut all the oranges in half and squeeze out the juice, then strain into a pan to remove the pulp. You'll need 160ml of strained juice in total. Add the zest of two oranges to the pan with the sugar and bring to a simmer, stirring to dissolve the sugar. Reduce the heat and simmer for 5–10 minutes until you have achieved a sticky syrup that is not caramelised. The liquid will be about three tablespoons (45ml) in total. Leave to cool.

Finish the dressing · Pour the orange syrup into a tall beaker suitable to use with a stick blender. Add the vinegar and water. Start blitzing, and then slowly pour the oil in in a steady stream. Add the yoghurt and lemon juice and blend again until smooth. Add the zest of half an orange. Pour the dressing into a jar and chill in the fridge for up to 1 week, but I think that this is best used immediately. If you store it, before you use it make sure to add a tablespoon of warm water and shake or blend until emulsified.

HONEY MUSTARD VINAIGRETTE

85g wholegrain mustard
110ml white wine vinegar
60g honey
5g salt
½ tsp cracked black pepper
600ml sunflower oil
10ml water

MAKES 800ML

This is so quick to make – it's sharp, sweet and peppery and will lift any salad.

Make the vinaigrette · Put the mustard, vinegar, honey, salt and pepper in a large bowl, then whisk to combine. Gradually pour in the oil until it's emulsified. Finally, whisk in the water and transfer to a jar. Chill for up to 6 weeks and use as required.

LEMON MAYONNAISE

4 egg yolks
1 tsp Dijon mustard
2 tsp white wine vinegar
2 tsp salt
½ tbsp caster sugar
300ml vegetable oil
50ml extra virgin olive oil
80ml warm water
finely grated zest of 3 lemons
    (on a Microplane)
90ml lemon juice

MAKES 600ML

This is a little thinner than normal mayonnaise, but it's super fresh because of the zest and juice.

Make the mayonnaise · Put the egg yolks in a food processor with the mustard, vinegar, salt and sugar. Pour the vegetable and olive oils into a jug, then very slowly, little by little, add it to the egg mixture with the machine switched on. Halfway through, add the warm water to the food processor, mixing all the time until you have achieved a smooth, creamy texture.
Flavour the mayonnaise · Mix the lemon zest and juice into the mayonnaise and transfer to a clean jar. Store for up to 2 weeks in the fridge. Use as required.

MISO MAYONNAISE

110g peanut butter
50g white miso
2 egg yolks
215g lemon mayonnaise (page 247)
30g toasted sesame oil
juice and zest of 1 lime
15ml warm water

MAKES 400G

Kitchen Note: if you don't have the lemon mayonnaise, use normal mayonnaise and just add some lemon zest.

This simple mayo with Asian influences is great with fish or anything deep-fried.

Make the mayonnaise · Put the peanut butter in a large bowl with the miso and egg yolks, then whisk to combine. Add the lemon mayonnaise and sesame oil and whisk again until smooth. Finally, whisk in the lime juice and zest with the warm water, then transfer to a clean jar and chill for up to 1 week.

SALTED CARAMEL BUTTER SAUCE

200g granulated sugar
30g water
120ml double cream
85g unsalted butter
2 tsp sea salt flakes

MAKES ABOUT 350G

This is great with ice cream – it reminds me of being a kid.

Make the caramel · Heat a heavy-based pan over a medium heat. Add the sugar and water and heat until the sugar has dissolved. Increase the heat and continue to cook, without stirring, until the mixture has turned to a golden-brown caramel, swirling the pan occasionally to ensure the mixture caramelises evenly.

Make the sauce · Remove from the heat and beat in the cream, butter and salt until smooth and shiny. Leave to cool completely, then pour into a jar and store in the fridge for up to 3 weeks. Use as required, and serve warm or cold.

CARAMEL CHOCOLATE SAUCE

180g dark chocolate (at least
    70% cocoa solids)
200g caster sugar
130ml water
240ml cream
1 tsp vanilla extract
1 tsp sea salt flakes

MAKES ABOUT 700G

This sauce has a nice runny consistency and can be used hot or cold on ice cream, pancakes or waffles. It's my go-to on a cheat day.

Melt the chocolate · Break the chocolate into a heatproof bowl and set over a pan of simmering water until melted, stirring occasionally. Remove from the heat and stir until smooth.

Make the caramel · Heat a heavy-based pan over a medium heat. Add the sugar and water, and heat until the sugar has dissolved, brushing down the sides of the pan with a pastry brush dipped in water to prevent crystallising. Increase the heat and continue to cook, without stirring, until the mixture has turned to a golden-brown caramel, swirling the pan occasionally to ensure the mixture caramelises evenly.

Make the sauce · Remove from the heat and beat in the cream, vanilla and flaky salt until smooth and shiny. Remove from the heat, fold in the melted chocolate and stir until smooth. Leave to cool completely, then pour into a jar and store in the fridge for up to 1 month. Use as required and serve warm or cold.

VANILLA STOCK SYRUP

1 vanilla pod
500g sugar
1 litre water
1 strip orange peel (from a
    speed peeler)
1 strip lemon peel (from a
    speed peeler)

MAKES 1.5 LITRES

This is so handy to have in the kitchen for making desserts. A few spoonfuls will add a hint of sweetness. It's perfect for poaching fruit and also a great alternative to sugar, with a bit more depth.

Make the syrup · Cut the vanilla pod in half and then scrape out the seeds. Put both in a pan with the sugar, water and orange and lemon peels over a medium heat. Bring to the boil, then reduce the heat and simmer for a few minutes, stirring occasionally, until the sugar has dissolved and you have a clear syrup. Remove from the heat and leave to cool down. Pour into a clean jar.
Store the syrup · Store in the fridge. This stock syrup will last for up to a year.

ACKNOWLEDGEMENTS

Firstly, I'd like to thank the fathers and their loved ones who bought this book. For all those who cherish the responsibility of family and all that it entails, I hope you find joy in this book.

A big 'thank you' to Billy, my right-hand man, for all that you do.

To Pierre, who worked alongside me on this challenge.

To Orla and Leo, who styled and shot the photographs, for their great work and professionalism.

To Sarah, Aoibheann and Orla, and all the team at Gill for giving this idea life.

And a special 'thank you' to past head chefs in the restaurants – Bernard, Daniel Cl., Al, Boris, Tomas, Laxman – for their commitment and dedication over the years. Some have become fathers now in their own right.

Finally, to my brothers and sister – Francis, Colin, Mary and Patrick – for your love and loyalty. It's been a pleasure watching you all grow.

And to my son, Oscar. And also to Ryan, Jack, Bobby, Sonny and Polly. What a team! Look after each other.

INDEX